BE
HOLY

BE HOLY

FIND IDENTITY
FIND BELONGING
FIND PURPOSE

BRIAN CHRISTOPHER COULTER

CHALICE
PRESS

ST. LOUIS, MISSOURI

www.ChalicePress.com

Print: 9780827202931   EPUB: 9780827202948   EPDF: 9780827202955

Library of Congress Cataloging-in-Publication Data

Coulter, Brian Christopher.
 Be holy : find identity, find belonging, find purpose / Brian Christopher Coulter.
-- First [edition].
    pages cm
 ISBN 978-0-8272-0293-1 (pbk.)
 1. Christian life. I. Title.

BV4501.3.C68925 2014
248.4—dc23
                          2014037135

Printed in the United States of America

This book is dedicated to
my Megan,
my girls,
my sister, my mother, my father,
and all the other saints who made it possible.

contents

preface

First Peter states, "Be holy yourselves in all your conduct; for it is written, 'You shall be holy, for I am holy.'"[1] What do you think it means to be holy? We find it again in Ephesians when we read that God "chose us in Christ before the foundation of the world to be holy."[2] And in the last chapter of the last book of the Bible we read, "Let the evildoer still do evil, and the filthy still be filthy, and the righteous still do right, and the holy still be holy."[3]

The command to "be holy" echoes throughout scripture and should be understood as a challenge to live our lives differently. Over and over we read passages in which God calls us to repent or turn from what we know and reorient our lives in a new direction. God calls us to be holy—to orient our lives in a new direction—to be set apart for, with, and from.

This is where it gets fascinating to me. People seem to get confused about why we are called to be holy. We are not called to be holy for God. God does not need us to accomplish God's purpose in this world. God is God. God can do anything with or without us. God does not benefit from us choosing to be holy…we do. We are the ones who benefit from being holy.

Living a "normal" life today can lead us to frustration, disappointment, and empty overindulgence. Differentiating yourself from the "normal" crowd is often a very good thing. We are not invited to be holy because God needs worker drones; God invites us to be holy because it is a better way for us to experience and live life. When we make the choice to be holy, we find a richer, fuller existence. When we make that choice, we find satisfaction for cravings we did not even know we had. When we choose to live a holy life, we are choosing to live the way we were created to live.

This book will primarily be for young adults—the "missing age group" in many churches. Mainline Protestant denominations often lose young adults during college, and only a few of them find their way back when they reproduce and want their children to be baptized. They vanish. They are absent from our communities. I do not think this is due to their failure as Christians. I think this is our failure as the church.

Three things that we are all searching for as we transition from youth to adulthood are identity, belonging, and purpose.[4] We want to know who we are, where we belong, and why we are here. Unfortunately, our churches do not always help us with this search. The church is much better at saying what it stands against than what it stands for.[5] Rather than focusing on who-what-why we are, the church all too often points to who we should not be and what we should not do, all the while hoping that we never ask, "Why not?"

This is why scholars say Moralistic Therapeutic Deism is so pervasive within our congregations.[6] It is a diluted form of religion which professes that all we need to do is live a pretty good life and play nice with others so that God will take care of us. The problem with this line of thinking is that good and bad things happen in life regardless of your ethics or church affiliation. The world does not revolve around you and it is not solely focused on your happiness. God is not a divine vending machine dispensing to us whatever we think we need at any given moment.

So why should young adults come to church if the church is failing to help them transition into adulthood and telling them a lie?

In this book, speaking for the church as a young adult, I address these issues as I remind us of our calling to "be holy." And while this book is primarily for young adults, it is for anyone struggling with who they are, where they belong, and why they are here. It is for anyone looking for a better way of life. It is for anyone seeking to expose flimsy, insipid faith and reveal true, authentic Christianity. It is really for everyone. This book is dedicated to fleshing out what it means to be holy and how we can find and develop our sense of identity, belonging, and purpose through this invitation.

our calling…
be holy

chapter 1—yearning

"I can't believe that God put us on this earth to be ordinary."
— *Lou Holtz*

"...so that they may take hold of the life that really is life."
—*1 Timothy 6:19*

*"If I find in myself desires which nothing in the world can satisfy,
the only logical explanation is that I was made for another world."*
—*C.S. Lewis*

I like art. I have nothing against art. I am pretty good with chalk on a sidewalk and I took ceramics in college. I simply do not always understand art.

I remember an awkward conversation with a friend after he showed me one of his paintings. The painting was sitting on an easel and it was "abstract" to say the least. I took one look at it and was confused. I tried to act like I was not and I tried to be encouraging. I told him it was great. The colors were vibrant and his technique was impressive. But then I asked a question—a very silly question. As I pointed to an empty space on the canvas, I asked: "What are you going to put there?"

As it turns out, he was not going to put anything there. He was finished. He was also very insulted. #oops

I did not think I was seeing the final product. I viewed the painting and thought it was a great start, but something was missing. I have this same thought when I look at most sculptures. Sculptors, more than any other artists, like to mess with our minds. There are so many sculptures out there without limbs or heads or pieces you would expect to be there.

When I come across one that appears to be unfinished I think back to my experience with my friend and the empty space on the canvas and I ask myself, "Is something missing, or am I missing something?"

Is something missing from this piece of art? Is something unfinished? Is something absent?

Or am I missing something? Do I simply not understand? Am I unable to see what is meant to be seen?

This is not just in art. This is in life.

Is something missing from our lives? Are we lacking something? Is there an absence of something? Is there an absence of someone? Do we feel incomplete? Is something missing, or are we missing something? Is there something happening that we are not aware of? Do we not understanding what is right in front of us? Are we missing something?

Is something really missing in our lives, or are we just missing something?

A few years ago, the Washington Post conducted a social experiment during a Washington, D.C., rush hour. A guy simply exited the metro at the L'Enfant Plaza station, stood alone next to a trash bin, took out a violin, and began to play.

He played the violin for 43 minutes. As people walked by he got a few glances. He received some spare change, but for the most part people just pretended he was not there. The overwhelming majority of people completely ignored him on that day. The few who did stop to listen to him were almost all curious children who were then dragged away by their hurried parents.

The irony with this social experiment was that the man playing was actually a violinist named Joshua Bell. Bell was a child prodigy who at the age of 4 would play classical music by ear on rubber bands by stretching and varying the tones. Now thirty-nine years old, Bell is one of the world's finest violinists. A few nights before this social experiment, Bell sold out Boston's stately Symphony Hall where decent tickets cost around $100. A couple of weeks later, Bell would play to a standing-room-only audience so respectful of his artistry that they were silent to the point of stifling their coughs.

At the L'Enfant Plaza station next to the trash bin, Bell was playing some of the world's finest musical arrangements. He played some Bach, some Schubert, some Manuel Ponce. Bell was also using one of the finest instruments ever made. The violin Bell used was handcrafted in 1713 by

Antonio Stradivari during the Italian master's "golden period" and was purchased for around 3.5 million dollars.

Is something really missing from our lives, or are we just missing something? One of the greatest musicians, playing one of the best instruments, playing some of the greatest music ever written was totally and completely missed by well over a thousand people.[1] No crowd gathered. No applause was given. No appreciation was offered.

How many other amazing things are out there that we miss? How often do you listen to the words of those around you without hearing the wisdom in them? How often do you watch things without truly seeing their beauty? How often do you feel someone touching you without any feeling of connection?

Maybe the thing we are missing most in life is awareness.

***

My wife and I recently went through a program called Financial Peace University. It is one of Dave Ramsey's courses dealing with money and debt and budgets and what it means to live a "normal life."

In his program, Dave Ramsey says over and over again that he does not want to be normal. Seven out of ten people in the United States live paycheck to paycheck. Seventy percent is the majority. Seventy percent makes it normal. This means that if we were to miss one paycheck, some of our bills would go unpaid. This means that if we were to miss one paycheck, we would fall behind. This means that if we miss one paycheck, then we continue the cycle of drowning in our debt.

This is normal. This is how the majority of Americans live. We spend more than we have. The average credit card debt in a household that has credit card debt is $15,956.[2] We have this empty, incomplete feeling. We want more. We yearn for more. So we swipe the card in an attempt to fill the void in our lives and we become further and further behind. This, unfortunately, is normal.

Dave says: "I don't want to be normal, because normal is broke."[3]

I agree with this. Normal is broke. Normal is careless. Normal is wasteful. Normal is overindulgence. But this is not just a financial problem—this is a life problem.

Normal is living your life in a careless, thoughtless, unintentional way. It is waking up in the morning without a purpose. It is going to bed at night wondering where the day went. It is allowing your days, your years, your life to casually slip away.

Normal is being wasteful of your talents, gifts, abilities, resources, connections, and relationships. It is refusing to accept who you are. It is taking the easy way. It is following the safe path. It is avoiding what seems difficult. It is limiting rather than developing your potential. It is failure to live your life to the fullest.

Normal is overindulgence that leads to greed, gluttony, and a hunger that can quickly get out of control. It is consuming at the expense of others. It is chasing the wrong things. Normal values consumption over completeness. It is wanting more while giving less. It is merely existing rather than truly living.

I don't want to be normal.

Normal is broke.

Normal is broken.

***

We all have guiding principles in life. We all have ways in which we navigate this world. We learn and develop and grow into these ways and principles throughout our lives. Some call this our ideology or philosophy. Others call it faith or religion. But for now, we are going to refer to it as a worldview. It is our particular way in which we view the world.

Our worldview is our lens through which we perceive what happens around us. This lens allows us to focus in on certain aspects of life as well as filter out the distractions and haze around us.

My sister is a photographer with a fancy camera and the expensive lenses to go with it. We took a family vacation to Disney World last year and we spent quite a bit of time trying to get the perfect shot of us with the giant Epcot "golfball" in the background. This proved to be more difficult than we imagined. When we took the picture it seemed that either we were in focus and the ball was fuzzy or we were a blur and the ball appeared in great detail. So eventually we had to decide what we more important to us. What did we want to focus on in the picture? What were some of the details we could filter out of the picture?

Our worldview helps us focus.

Our worldview helps us filter.

Our worldview helps us to focus on what is important to us. The lens we use to view the world shapes what we notice in the world. If you are an optimist, the world often appears to be a bright place. If you are a pessimist, the world probably seems a little gloomier to you. If you are a romantic, you can find joy and love in odd places. If you are a cynic, you will find doubt and uncertainty everywhere. The worldview through which you approach the world shapes the way you see it.

Our worldview also helps us filter through our perceptions. William James once famously said our world is "one great blooming, buzzing confusion."[4] If you were to freeze any moment in time and count everything happening to us or around us, it would never end. There are literally millions of things happening to us, in us, through us, around us at any given moment. If our senses did not filter any of this out, we would explode.

Think of the things that happen in your life that you no longer notice: The constant contact between your skin and your clothing. The soft hum of electronics. The scent of your deodorant. The taste of air. These things are so common and mundane that we learn to ignore them. We learn to filter them out so that we can focus elsewhere. So we can focus on the uncommon and unusual, so we can focus on what we deem to be important.

This is what our worldview does for us. It helps us understand what is significant and what is insignificant. It helps us determine what we do and do not notice. Our worldview shapes what we experience and encounter in life.

This is where we begin to differ. This is where our perceptions of the world become unique. No one has the same worldview as anyone else. No one focuses and filters the same way. Some take this to the extreme and are tempted to think we are so different from each other that we share nothing in common. Not true. We are a sea of similarities with drops of differences.

Our differences are real, however. We do look at things differently. We have unique perspectives on the world because we are uniquely positioned in this world. Only you can be you. Only you can view the world as you.

Think about growing up. Think about your background. Think about the experiences in your life that have brought you here…to this place… to this book…to this line of the book. None of us have had the same journey. None of us walk in with the same experiences. We all come at things from a slightly different angle. We all view the world through our unique worldview.

So our worldview helps us to focus and filter.

But can our worldview ever be detrimental to us?

Do we ever focus on the wrong things?

Do we ever filter out the extraordinary?

Do we ever stop to listen to the music at L'Enfant Plaza station?

***

Worldviews can change. They can be refocused. They can be set to filter differently. They can be expanded. Oliver Wendell Holmes is rumored to have said, "A mind, once stretched, can never return to its original condition."

This happens every day of our lives. Not always consciously, but it does take place. With every experience we have, with every sight we see, with every line we read—our worldview changes little by little.

A teacher of mine spent some time in an orphanage in Africa. The young children at that orphanage were typically left at the orphanage in bad health with little hope. The tiny infants left there were even worse off. Many of them were only weeks or days old and they were extremely malnourished.

The infants were starving to death—but lacking food was not the problem.

The orphanage had nourishment for those infants. They had formula and vitamins to give them. But they could not get the infants to take them. The problem was trying to convince those infants that they were starving to death. To those babies, starvation was normal. They had experienced nothing else. They had lived no other way.

So the volunteers at this orphanage would take sugar water and would place drops of it on the tongues of these infants. Drop after drop after drop they would give these calm, motionless, still babies. They were hoping for what most of us do not hope for. They were hoping for that child to cry. Not a soft, cute little cry for you to pick them up or burp them. They wanted an ear-shattering, world-splitting scream to come out of the mouths of these babies.

For when one of those infants began to scream like that, they knew she got it. The screaming meant that she was now aware of her hunger. The screaming meant that she was up for the struggle to feed for the first time. The screaming meant that she was now ready to fight for her life. The screaming meant that she had forever changed her definition of what life should be. The screaming meant she had shifted her worldview.

Is something missing, or are we missing something?

Are we yearning for something else, something better, something more?

Is there something in our lives that we need to start screaming about?

Do we need to shift our worldview?

***

Madonna is an artist, entertainer, singer, songwriter, actress, dancer, and entrepreneur. She has sold over 300 million records worldwide. She was recognized as one of the 25 Most Powerful Women of the Past Century by *Time* magazine and is in the Guinness Book of World Records for being the world's best-selling female recording artist of all time. Madonna is one of the few people in this world that does not need a second name. Madonna is doing pretty well for herself.

But even Madonna has had the feeling that something is off with her life. She has felt incomplete. She has felt insufficient. She has felt fragmented. After all she has done and after all she has accomplished, she still has felt inadequate.

In an interview with *Vanity Fair* a while back, Madonna said:

> I have an iron will and all of my will has always been devoted to conquering some horrible feelings of inadequacy. I'm always struggling with that fear. I push past one spell of it and discover myself as a special human being of worth and then I get to another stage and I think I'm mediocre and uninteresting and worthless and I have to find a way to get myself out of that again and again. My drive in life is from this horrible feeling of being inadequate and mediocre and it is always pushing me, and pushing me and pushing me. Because even though I have become somebody, I still have to prove that I am somebody. My struggle has never ended and it probably never will.[5]

This is a universal struggle with a universal pain that we have all felt.

In the honest and raw moments of our solitude, we all struggle. We struggle with feelings of inadequacy. We struggle with who we are. We struggle with who others are. We struggle with our relationships. We struggle with our fragmented lives. We struggle with what we do. We struggle with what we fail to do. We struggle with what we are unable to do. We all struggle.

We have all been tired, exhausted, and worn out from the struggle—wondering if it has to be this way or if there is an alternative, some relief, any hope in the midst of it all.

John Coltrane is one of the great jazz saxophonists and is known worldwide for his music. He spent his early career in the "bebop" expression of jazz, and later split off to create his own styles and expressions. Coltrane is known primarily for his music today, but after his death in 1967 the African Orthodox Church actually declared him to be Saint John William Coltrane for his dedication of faith and his walk with the Lord.

There is a story that emerged after one of John Coltrane's last performances, in which he played one of his famous songs entitled "A Love Supreme." As any performer will tell you, every performance is different and every performance is unique. This is especially true when it comes to jazz. The freedom to explore within the lines and melody make room for extremely different performances of the same piece. On this particular night, Coltrane played what many consider to be his greatest performance ever. And after his uninhibited extraordinary delivery of "A Love Supreme," he walked offstage, set down his saxophone, and spoke the holy words: *"nunc dimittis."*

Nunc dimittis comes from the Latin translation of the story of Simeon. Simeon was a devout and observant Jew who was alive the year at which we divide history. According to the gospel of Luke, God had spoken to Simeon and told him that he would not die until he had seen the Lord's Messiah. Simeon was getting old. Simeon was struggling with God's promise. Simeon was wondering if his life would ever be complete.

But then Simeon met Mary and Joseph and was able to hold their child, Jesus, in his arms. As he held the child, he thanked God and said *nunc dimittis*, or "now dismiss." Simeon was finished. Simeon's life was complete. Simeon was no longer struggling with anything. Simeon said:

> *Nunc dimittis servum tuum, Domine, secundum verbum tuum in pace:*
> *Quia viderunt oculi mei salutare tuum*
> *Quod parasti ante faciem omnium populorum:*
> *Lumen ad revelationem gentium, et gloriam plebis tuae Israel.*[6]
> Master, now you are dismissing your servant in peace,
>   according to your word;
> for my eyes have seen your salvation,
>   which you have prepared in the presence of all peoples,
> a light for revelation to the Gentiles
>   and for glory to your people Israel.[7]

Coltrane ended his 32-minute jazz prayer by asking God for a dismissal. Coltrane knew that his life, in that moment, was complete. He knew who he was, where he belonged, and why he was there. Coltrane felt as though his whole life had been building to, leading up, and growing towards that moment. Coltrane was now telling God: Lord, I have done what I needed to do, I have been where I needed to be, I have become who I needed to become. You have made me whole. My life is complete. I am ready to go. The struggle is over. *Nunc dimittis.*[8]

***

I am convinced that there is a better way to live life.

Too many people go through life without actually living it. They constantly live with a yearning for more of the wrong things. They welcome the status quo. They never challenge or question why things are the way they are. They consent to their feelings of inadequacy, isolation, and insignificance. They strive to be normal.

Why?

Why do we do this?

Why do we spend so much time trying to blend in when we were designed to stand out?

Why do we strive for ordinary when we are created extraordinary?

My worldview is a Christian worldview. I try to focus and filter my experience of life through the lens of Jesus. The way I organize and understand this world is profoundly shaped though what I encounter in scripture. This makes the Bible more than just *a* story. It makes the Bible *my* story.

But the Bible is not just mine. Scripture tells us *our* story—the story of God and God's people. God created us. God loves us. God approaches us. God lives for us. God dies for us. God is raised for us.

And it is in our story that we find our calling: be holy. This calling is introduced early in our story, emphasized throughout the poetry and the wisdom and prophecies of the Hebrew people, revealed in its fullest form in the person of Jesus, and reiterated in the letters of the early church. Over and over again we read these two little words.

Be holy—two little words that make up our calling.

Be holy—two little words that echo throughout our story.

Be holy—two little words that reveal another way to live life.

Be holy—two little words that reveal a better way to live life.

Be holy.

chapter 2—become

"It takes courage to grow up and become who you really are."
— *E.E. Cummings*

"So if anyone is in Christ, there is a new creation:
everything old has passed away; see, everything has become new!"
— *2 Corinthians 5:17*

"I must be willing to give up what I am in order
to become what I will be."
— *Albert Einstein*

I once watched a youth soccer coach give the welcoming address to new players and parents. He ended by slightly raising the volume of his voice and asking the kids, "Do you want to be soccer players?" He received a resounding "YES." His response: "That's great, but first you have to *become* a soccer player. Put on your cleats and let's get started."

The title of this book is *be holy*, not becoming holy. Nonetheless, we must first "become" before we can "be." So how are we made holy? What does it mean to become holy?

***

Is anyone else out there a Pinterest fan?

Pinterest is a website of virtual pinboards put on display for the world to see.[1] You could literally spend your entire day searching through all the pinboards they have. I know. I have.

The name "Pinterest" itself came from the combination of the words *pin* and *interest* People pin things that they find interesting on the World Wide Web. These pins are then organized in an aesthetically pleasing way that is easily searchable. I am pretty sure you could find anything you want to find on Pinterest.

Back in the day, when I was still living my pre-Pinterest life, I did not know the extent of the human obsession with DIY (do-it-yourself). I knew it existed. I knew people like to do things themselves. But I did not understand how fixated we were as a culture with DIY projects.

DIY projects are all over Pinterest: DIY crafts. DIY patios. DIY Christmas ornaments. DIY lettuce wraps. DIY anything you could imagine. I am convinced that DIY are the most popular three-letters on Pinterest.

A few months ago my aunt taught me how to make salsa and I have not bought premade salsa since. In fact, every gathering, football game, or celebration I go to I bring my DIY salsa. There is a part of making something on your own that makes you feel good. For every compliment I get, I pat myself on the back a little more.

I take my salsa so often and talk about it so much that someone actually gave me my own jalapeno plant. So now I grow my own jalapenos for my salsa. Now that is DIY!!

We like to do things ourselves. We enjoy a sense of accomplishment. We want to achieve. We want to triumph. We want success.

My oldest daughter is getting to the point at which she can put on her own shoes. This is *huge* for her. Not only can she put them on, but she can go pick out which pair to wear, get them out of her drawer, sit down, and complete her quest all by herself. When she walks out she is beaming with pride and waiting for praise. Chances are about 50/50 that her shoes are on the wrong feet, but nevertheless her feet are covered.

This is true in all aspects of life, at all ages of life: The gardener who transforms his yard. The surgeon waiting for her first solo surgery. The gamer who wants discover the crystal wand without the cheat codes. DIY projects provide us with a sense of winning. It is appealing and attractive to do-it-yourself (or at least to have done-it-yourself).

Recently this has even become true for spirituality. We want to make spirituality happen for us. We want to become spiritual on our own. We want spirituality to be our fun, new DIY project for this Saturday. There has been and continues to be a whole "spiritual but not religious" movement. People want to be spiritual. They want to feel a connection to something beyond themselves. They want to explore this idea of the divine. They just do not want to do this as a part of a religious institution.

They want to be free to discover as they wish. They want to make it a solo journey. They want to do it on their own.

Many of us think of holiness in similar terms to spirituality. Holiness is a part of our spiritual journey. Our quest for holiness becomes like our quest for spirituality. There is nothing wrong with this connection, but with the recent emphasis on being "spiritual but not religious" it might lead to some misunderstandings. We might begin to think in terms of DIY holiness. We might try to make holiness a private, silent endeavor that we do on our own.

Can we make holiness?

Can we become holy on our own?

Is it really that simple?

***

Some scriptures might appear to support this idea of DIY holiness. Leviticus 20 states: "Consecrate yourselves therefore, and be holy."[2] At the root of the word "consecrate" is the word "holy." Simply translated, "consecrate" means "to make holy." So in essence, this verse is telling you to "make yourselves holy, and be holy."

Step one, make yourself holy.

Step two, be holy.

Step three, write a book about it.

#nailedit

Is that really the intent of the passage, though? Are we to believe that holiness is truly that easy and formulaic?

We all approach scripture with baggage—some good, some bad—but we all bring our own knowledge, experience, questions, problems, and anxieties with us when we approach the Bible. Problems arise when we begin to read our own baggage into scriptures and we begin to look for what we want them to say. Too often we go to scripture with the wrong questions rather than simply listening for God's right answers.

That is why it is good to remember that each passage or verse or chapter is simply a part of the larger narrative of the Bible. These words, "Consecrate yourselves therefore, and be holy," were spoken by God through Moses to the Israelites as they were camped in the wilderness at the foot of Mount Sinai. The story does not start here. Anytime you go to the Bible and do not start reading in Genesis 1, you have to realize you are not starting at the beginning of our story.

The Israelites were slaves in Egypt until God freed them and led them out via the parted Red Sea. God provided them with water to drink in the middle of the desert. God gave them manna and quail to eat when there was no food around. God protected them from their attackers when they were helpless and unable. God did all of this for them and then led them to the point at which they hear these words: "Consecrate yourselves therefore, and be holy."

The Israelites had no illusion that they could have done this all themselves. The Israelites knew that they were a dependent people. Now sometimes they forgot who they were dependent upon…but that is another story.

For us to read these words and make holiness into our next DIY project is not only an abuse of scripture, but is a gross misunderstanding of how it is that we become holy. I do not have that much faith in you. I do not have that much faith in myself. I have seen some of the bad things men and women have done. I have witnessed my own fallen nature. We cannot make ourselves holy.

But this is not the only verse related to holiness that people twist in odd ways. Isolating verses and looking for the quick, simple, black-or-white answer gets very confusing very quickly. Many of these scriptures actually leave me with more questions than answers.

Luke 2 states plainly, "Every firstborn male shall be designated as holy to the Lord."[3] So is this saying that you have to be a firstborn male to be holy? Is it birth order that makes us holy? Is it our sex? Is it some sort of combination? Is becoming holy a matter of winning the genetic lottery?

First Corinthians 7 seems to suggest that holiness could be about making the right spousal selection or by choosing your parents wisely. We read, "The unbelieving husband is made holy through his wife, and the unbelieving wife is made holy through her husband. Otherwise, your children would be unclean, but as it is, they are holy."[4] So are we made holy by our spouse? Are we made holy by our parents? What if you are single? What if you are an orphan? As a side note, I am pretty sure that my children would be unclean without my wife—she is much more consistent with bath time than I am.

Exodus 29 is about holiness and clothing choices. It is less about the clothing itself, but more about what you put on your clothing. "Then you shall take some of the blood that is on the altar, and some of the anointing oil, and sprinkle it on Aaron and his vestments and on his sons and his sons' vestments with him; then he and his vestments shall be holy, as well as his sons and his sons' vestments."[5] Is it the clothes you wear and how you wear them that make you holy? Could holiness ever become trendy? I wonder what Aaron used to get the stains out.

Is becoming and staying holy directly related to your hairstyle? Numbers 6: "All the days of their nazirite vow no razor shall come upon the head; until the time is completed for which they separate themselves to the Lord, they shall be holy."[6] Should you get your hair cut? Should you let it grow out for a while? What about the split ends?

Is it the food we offer that makes us holy? Leviticus 21 states: "You shall treat them as holy, since they offer the food of your God; they shall be holy to you, for I the Lord, I who sanctify you, am holy."[7] Or is it how we offer the food that we offer that makes us holy? "They shall be holy to their God…for they offer the LORD's offerings by fire, the food of their God; therefore they shall be holy."[8]

What do all these verses really say about holiness?

Can we achieve holiness through gender, birth order, parental control, spousal selection, clothing choices, hairstyle, or fire-roasted food offerings?

Is this all the Bible has to say about it?

We read books with my daughter every night as a part of her bedtime routine. She picks them out. We normally give her freedom of choice to select two books, but there are some caveats. She knows that Daddy will whine if she picks out a Barbie book and that Mommy will read a lot more than just two stories if she picks out her Children's Bible Storybook. She already knows how to circumnavigate the system.

Recently, she has been picking out one of the same books over and over. It tells the fable of the blind mice who encounter an elephant—but they do not yet know what it is. The first mouse runs into a leg and tells the other mice they have encountered a pillar. A second mouse runs into the trunk and claims it is a snake. Other mice find the ear, head, and tail, then separately report that they believe it is a fan, a cliff, and a vine. Finally the last mouse runs into the elephant and explores the entire animal, running from side to side and all around it. That last mouse understands where each of the other mice drew their conclusions, but also realizes that they were not encountering the entire animal. That last mouse invites all the other mice to come and explore the animal with him so that they can all discover and agree that it is in fact an elephant. The book ends with,

"The Mouse Moral: knowledge in part is fine, but wisdom comes from seeing the whole."

We cannot encounter one verse or a small collection of passages in the Bible about holiness and pretend that this is all the Bible has to say about it. The Bible can be twisted and used to support some really weird stuff if you approach it in this way. We must remember the larger narrative. We must explore our whole story.

I do not believe we can make ourselves holy. While isolating a few select verses may direct our attention toward DIY holiness, I do not think this is their intent, or what the whole of scripture seems to emphasize. Scripture is bigger than these verses. Scripture says more than just this. The beauty of the Bible is that you can go to it time and time again and continue to find more than you found last time. It is full of timeless truths and fresh insights. It is always dangerous for us to simply look at a few verses and proclaim with bold assurance that we know exactly what God has to say on any subject.

But if we don't make ourselves holy, who does?

***

Phyllis Tickle once preached these words:

> We're hearing more and more about the fact that all religions are the same, that all religions go to the same place, that all religions are very alike, that probably they all speak to the same God. And they differ from each other simply because they are in different cultural contexts. There is a degree of truth that says that most religions share a common wisdom; that is to say, we want the same things for humanity, we believe in some of the same moral values—that's absolutely true. But, religions differ in their mysteries.[9]

One of the ways Christianity is different is our claim that God came down to earth and took on human flesh. Jesus of Nazareth, fully God, came into our world in the same way we did and became fully human—fully God, fully human, fully realized in Jesus. The arithmetic on that sentence is mind-boggling. It is an enigma. It is a mystery.

More mysterious than that statement is what Christians believe comes to us through Jesus. In Jesus, we believe that God reaches into humanity, bridges the gap between us, and invites us into a relationship of forgiveness and mercy. That invitation to a relationship is a gift. It is not something that we earned. It is not something we could initiate. The opportunity to enter into that kind of a relationship with God is a God-given gift to us and is unique to Christianity.

Through that relationship, we are granted grace.

Through that relationship, we are given new life.

Through that relationship, we are offered holiness.

Jesus says these words to some of his earliest followers: "I am the vine, you are the branches."[10] Jesus is all about making life easy to understand. Jesus is all about helping us see the complexities of the world in and through our everyday lives. A vine is something these disciples could see, touch, and hold. A vine was something they could wrap their minds around. Jesus, calling himself the vine and them the branches, is giving them a way to visualize their relationship. The vine goes into the ground and develops roots to sustain and nourish the entire plant.

The vine is what gives life to the rest of the plant. The branch is ultimately connected to the vine for survival. Without that relationship, the branch could not survive. The branch is enabled to produce solely because it is connected to something beyond itself. Without that connection, without that relationship, the branch is useless and lifeless. But with that relationship to the vine, the branch can thrive. The branch can grow, explore, and mature when it is attached. The branch experiences life through the vine. The branch benefits simply through its relationship and connection to the vine.

The letter written to the early church in Rome picks up on this notion of being a branch. In Romans 11 we read: "if the root is holy, then the branches also are holy."[11] If the root is holy, holiness flows to the rest of the plant. When a vine is rooted with holiness, then the branches feel the effects.

We the branches are made holy through Jesus the vine.

Christianity boldly asserts that we are rooted in God's holiness through Jesus. So to those who still tend to think in terms of DIY holiness, it seems that we have very little say in the matter of becoming holy. We are just recipients of holiness through our relationship with Jesus.

Ephesians 1 states that God "chose us in Christ before the foundation of the world to be holy and blameless before him in love."[12] Way before we were born, way before we were even a thought in our parents' or grandparents' heads, we were chosen in Christ to be holy.

We, as Christians, might not always be great at following Christ. We might not always live up to being chosen. We might mess up. We might hesitate, falter, or fall completely flat in our relationship with God. But God is still for us. God is still with us. Colossians 1 reads, "And you who were once estranged and hostile in mind, doing evil deeds, he has now reconciled in his fleshly body through death, so as to present you holy and blameless and irreproachable before him."[13] It is through the cross that we are reconciled to God. It is through the cross we are reminded of being chosen. It is through the cross we find our holiness.

We read something similar in the first letter to the Corinthians: "That is what some of you used to be! But you were washed clean, you were made holy to God, and you were made right with God in the name of the Lord Jesus Christ and in the Spirit of our God."[14] It is not through our own actions. It is through God's actions. Earlier in the same letter we read: "It is because of God that you are in Christ Jesus. He became wisdom from God for us. This means that he made us righteous and holy, and he delivered us. This is consistent with what was written: The one who brags should brag in the Lord!"[15] We become holy through Jesus. We are made holy through God. This is not something to boast about. It is something to be humbled by.

So God is the agent. God is the one acting. It is God who makes us holy. Holiness is not something we accomplish or achieve. Holiness is a gift we have been given.

***

If you ever want to make a lot of comic book fans mad at you, make up a new series about a superhero's adolescence. Welcome to CW network's television show *Smallville*.

In this series, Clark Kent is still young. He is transitioning into adulthood. He is growing into his identity. Clark Kent has all of his superpowers, but does not always know what to do with them. He is still figuring this out. He is still discovering their purpose.

The struggle for Clark Kent is not in becoming someone who has superpowers; it is about embracing his superpowers. It is about embracing the gifts he has been given. It is about embracing his destiny to be Superman.

This is us with holiness. Our choice seems to be less about becoming holy and more about embracing holiness.

The fancy church words for this are *justification* and *sanctification*. Justification is all about *becoming* holy. Justification is the work of God *on* us. Sanctification is all about *being* holy. Sanctification is the work of God *in* us. The Spirit frees us, delivers us, and liberates us in justification so that God can transform us, shape us, and mold us in sanctification. Sanctification is God indwelling in us, turning us back toward God, and enabling us to love, live, give, and grow in Christ. Sanctification is a process. Sanctification is about progress.

While justification and sanctification are separate, they are closely related. While becoming holy and being holy are different, they are intimately connected.

Holiness does not come from us. Holiness is not perfected by us. Holiness does not begin or end with us. Holiness is a gift we have been given and a gift we should embrace.

The author of 1 Peter is quoting Leviticus when we read: "Be holy yourselves in all your conduct; for it is written, 'You shall be holy, for I am holy.'"[16] The verb "be" reveals a lot in this passage. It tells us how we can embrace holiness. It indicates to us what we should expect on our journey toward holiness. It is not easily seen in the English translation, but it is definitely there in the original Greek.

In the English language we mainly think of verbs as representing the time of the action. We think of verbs in terms of past, present, or future. This is not the case for all languages. This word "be" is our English translation of the Greek verb *ginomai*, and the Greek language looks at verbs in a slightly different way. In Greek, verbs primarily represent the *kind* of action that is taking place rather than the *time* the action took place.

There are different categories of verbs in Greek depending on the kind of action they represent. There are simple-occurrence verbs that represent a one-time event (e.g., getting a high-five). There are completed verbs, which are one-time events that have lingering effects (e.g., getting married). Then there are continuous verbs, which are verbs that are constant, endless, and that just keep going.

Our verb *ginomai* ("be") is a continuous verb.[17] It shows an action in progress. It shows a state of persistence. It is a constant, endless action that just keeps going.

We cannot choose to be holy and be done. Holiness is not a goal that we will ever fully achieve. Holiness does not have an end-point. Holiness will never be checked off your list. Holiness is a continual pursuit.

***

An African metaphor about farms may help us understand holiness as a continual pursuit.[18]

In America, farms have fences. They hold the animals. They keep the livestock contained. So the question in America to determine if the animals are where they need to be is: "Are the animals inside or outside of the fence?" Once this is determined, the question is answered and over.

In Africa, farms usually do not have fences. There is nothing other than people to herd and keep the animals. So the question in Africa is not where the animals are in relation to the fence, but in relation to the farm. "Are the animals heading toward the farm or away from it?" This question does not end. This question is continually asked and continually answered. This question is never over.

Being holy is not about fences. It is not about being inside or outside the holiness fence. Being holy is about moving in the direction of holiness. Are we heading toward holiness? Or are we heading away from it?

Be holy.

Embrace holiness.

Head toward holiness.

chapter 3—reflection

"You shall be holy, for I the Lord your God am holy"
— Leviticus 19:2

"What we do comes out of who we believe we are."
— Rob Bell

"If you don't stand for something you will fall for anything."
— Malcolm X

Bath time in our house is an event—two little girls splashing and squirming in the tub as we try to introduce soap and shampoo into the watery chaos. My wife and I are usually soaked and drained at the end of the ordeal. One night as our indoor water park was closing, I said to my eldest, "Come on, let's hop out of the tub. Time to get pajamas on." She looked at me and said, "I can't, Daddy. I can't hop out of the tub."

My daughter is often stubborn. And when she is stubborn my wife often says: "She didn't get that from me."

So I repeated myself. A little slower and with more intentionality, I said to my daughter, "Come on. Let's hop out of the tub. Time to get pajamas on." She noticed the change in my pace and tone, so she too slowed down and made direct eye contact when she said: "I cannot do it, Daddy. I cannot hop out of the tub."

This was followed by a long silence…

I stared at her…

She stared at me...

I refused to be the first to break the silence….

(Maybe I am too stubborn…)

23

Finally, my four-year-old little girl spoke up and said: "I can't hop out of the tub, Daddy. I can't jump that high." She thought I literally wanted her to "hop" out of the tub. When, in actuality, I just wanted her to stand up so I could help her out of the tub. #LittleMissCommunication

(To keep you all up-to-date, my eldest daughter is big enough now to literally jump in and out of the tub by herself. That is a whole other separate dangerous issue we face now. Please say a little prayer for the safety of our household each night around 7:45 or so.)

I still remember the look of frustration and defeat on her face. "I can't, Daddy. I can't hop out of the tub. I can't jump that high." How often do we give up in life because of a misunderstanding? How often do we pout, quit, or become discouraged due to a lack of clarity?

Sadly, many Christians do this with the calling to be holy. They get frustrated because it seems too difficult. They give up because holiness seems unattainable. They ignore those verses in scripture that talk about holiness—because overlooking those passages seems easier than struggling with the meaning behind them.

We are not going to do this. We are not going to give up. We are not going to let the frustration get the best of us. We are not going to take the easy, more traveled, less rewarding path. We are not going to skip, ignore, or disregard holiness in the Bible.

So in the words of Isaiah 1: "Come now, let us reason together."[1]

***

The Hebrew Scriptures are also known as the Old Testament and are written in (you guessed it) Hebrew. The Hebrew word for "holy" is *qadash*. The New Testament was written in Greek. The Greek word for "holy" is *hagios*.

Now *qadash* and *hagios* are not always translated as "holy." "Holy" has all these variations, such as "holiness," "holies," and "holy-minded." It also shares its root with words such as "consecrate," "sanctify," and "saints." This does not mean that the meaning of *qadash* or *hagios* changes, but the context does.

When we read *qadash* or *hagios* in the future tense as an action verb ("to make holy"), it is usually just written as "consecrate." "Sanctify" is typically understood as "becoming holy." And "holy ones" is often translated as "saints." So even as the English translation of *qadash* or *hagios* changes in the context of how it is used, the root word remains "holy," and the base definition is always "to be set apart."[2]

To be holy is to be set apart.

But is that all that holiness is?

I currently reside in L.A. (Lower Alabama). Life is a little different here than in the places I have lived in the past. The pace of life is slower, the sunsets are a bit prettier, and the memorial service traditions are slightly different.

There is a company not too far from where I live that offers an alternative opportunity to celebrate the life of a late avid outdoors person. They advertise that their service is cost-effective, the ecological footprint is virtually nonexistent, and now you can even prearrange their services in advance to help your family members through their emotional loss of you if interested.

What they do is take the ash from the cremated remains of your loved one and place it into live ammunition. You can order rifle or pistol cartridges and shotgun shells through their website. They will gladly discuss category and quantity of ammunition with you as well as the options when determining your caliber and gauge needs.

And I know what you are thinking… How will this affect the trajectory of the shot? But they promise that the ash does not have any side effects on rifling, the propellant, or the firearm.

The name of this company is "Holy Smoke."[3]

#holysmokeindeed

So my question is, What makes Holy Smoke holy? Holy Smoke definitely offers something that is "set apart" in many ways. It is set apart from the traditional ways of remembering your loved ones. It is set apart from the standard way of producing ammunition. It is set apart with the idea that the remembrance of a person should be similar to the life of that person. It is set apart as a unique opportunity for a unique community of people.

So Holy Smoke is set apart, but does that automatically make it holy? Do you just have to be different to be holy? Do you just have to be unique to be holy? Is that all that holiness is?

To be holy is to be set apart. But it is being set apart in a multifaceted, intentional, purposeful way revealed to us through our Holy God.[4]

Being holy has many aspects. Being set apart is multidimensional. The basic essentials behind it all involve multiple components. First, you are holy or set apart *from*. So intrinsic within the word "holy" is separateness. Second, you are holy or set apart *for*. So also contained within the word "holy" is intention. Third, you are holy or set apart *with*—there is a communal element to it.

To be holy is to be set apart *from* all that is not holy.

To be holy is to be set apart *for* all that is holy.

To be holy is to be set apart *with* all who are holy.

To be holy means you are set apart for, from, and with. This multilayered approach to being set apart is found when we read about holiness in the Bible. Leviticus 20 tells us: "You shall be holy to me because I, the Lord, am holy, and I have set you apart from the nations to be mine."[5]

In this one verse of scripture we see all these layers of holiness. We are to be set apart from all that is not holy. We are to be set apart from the nations, the people, and the customs of those who live their life apart from God. We are to be set apart for all that is holy. We are to be set apart for God, for God's purpose, for God's calling. We are to be set apart with all who are holy. The "you" at the beginning is plural. You all are to be set apart together with God and with God's people.

To be holy is to be set apart from the normal, for our Holy God, with all the saints.

Maybe that company should just call themselves "Set Apart Smoke" instead.

***

When looking at holiness, it is important to remember all the pieces that come with being set apart. If you look at being holy on just one level, you might forget about the rest. Most of the time when I see a misunderstanding of what it means to be holy, it comes from simply focusing too much on one aspect of holiness or overlooking the others. But, sometimes, it is just totally wrong altogether.

People try to use synonyms for "holy" and "holiness." They come up with words such as: "excellence," "faultless," "completeness," "wholeness." While these words might play a small part in the definition of what it means to "be holy," it is misleading to begin there. None of them fully explain or define what "holy" is. So while a simple game of word-association might be somewhat helpful, the meaning of the word "holy" is beyond a simple synonym.

Take "perfection" as an example. The "Holiness Movement" began back in the 1840s with an emphasis on the "Christian perfection" teaching.

It holds to the possibility that a person can live free of voluntary sin. So perfection quickly became a synonym for holiness.

Perfection is not the same as holiness. I do not believe we can be perfect. I do believe we can be holy. Perfection focuses on achievement and a destination. Holiness focuses on participation and development. Perfection draws our attention to what we do and how we do it, not necessarily to why we do it.

When asked to describe someone who is holy, people often picture secluded monks or religious hermits or people who seem to be totally withdrawn from the world. While they may be holy, you do not have to live that way to be holy. If we are to be holy as God is holy, we should remember that God is very present and active in this world. God is not secluded. God is not private. God is for all of us and with all of us. If the holiness of God is to be visible to all, why would we all withdraw into a holy convent? Maybe we need to stop imagining holy people floating in the clouds and start picturing them working in the trenches.

Many people outside the Christian worldview hear the word "holy" and think "judgmental" or "condemnatory." This is not and cannot be a part of God's definition of holiness. So this is not and cannot be a part of how we see our calling to be holy.

Being holy is also not a way to control God. No one blatantly says that they have the power to control God, but we act as if we do all the time. We say odd little prayers along the lines of: "God, if you just take care of this, then I will go to church next week," or, "Help me out with this one so I can help you out with that one," or, "If you provide me with live ammunition containing the remains of my departed hunting buddy, I promise I will never hunt out of season again."

Being holy is not a way of getting something out of God. This skewed understanding sneaks into our lives little by little. We begin to believe that anytime something good happens in our life, it is because we were good and God is rewarding us. And we begin to believe that anytime something bad happens in our life, it is because we were bad and God is punishing us. This is just not true. This is not the gospel. This is not Christianity. This is believing karma, rather than grace.

I do believe that being holy has its rewards, but they are the intrinsic kind, not the extrinsic kind. Being holy does not force God to give you things. Being holy is its own reward.

I spent some time working at a church in Kenya. This rewards mentality was one of the hardest concepts to talk about over there. The prosperity gospel is big in Kenya. Some preachers get up in fancy suits with big rings and gold chains to tell the people how God made them rich. They say God made them rich because they listened to God. They say God rewarded their good behavior. They say God compensated them for their obedience. They say, "And you too can have all of this...if you start to put a little more faith in God, a little more trust in your Savior, and a little more money in the offering plate."[6]

Being holy is not about governing God. It is not about controlling the portion allotted to you. Being holy is about living your life set apart from the prosperity gospel myth, for God, and with God's people.

Being holy is its own blessing. When we make the choice to be holy we find satisfaction for cravings we did not even know we had. When we make the choice to be holy we discover who we are, where we belong, and why we are here. When we make the choice to be holy we find a richer, fuller existence. When we make the choice to be holy we find a life that is worth living.

***

The word "holy" itself is used a lot in the Bible. It is most often used to refer to God; sometimes used to refer to people, objects, events, or days; and occasionally used as a command or invitation. To best understand what the Christian understanding of holiness is all about, we should look at how the term is most often used. Using "holy" in relation to God tells us that God is set apart—but what does this mean?

Walter Brueggemann—author, scholar, and Old Testament trivia champion—points out that "holy" is the only term in the Old Testament referring to God that is not an analogy or metaphor.[7] It is not something the Israelites draw from their own life. It is not a description we give to God. "Holy" is a description God gives to God. This is God's term. God is the first one to use it. This means the best way to understand "holy" is to look to God. Holiness is wrapped up in who God is.

Our Holy God is set apart in many ways. God is set apart from the world. God is set apart from other gods. God is set apart from the temporary, the provisional, the impermanent. The holiness of God, the characteristic of God being holy, is about God being set apart from creation.

In the ancient world when scripture was first written, this was not always the belief. It was common for other tribes and peoples to hold to the belief that the divine lived in, through, and as a part of creation. This shaped the way they saw the world. This shaped the way they understood what was holy. Holiness for them was not set apart from anything. Holiness was not even set to the side of anything. Holiness was woven into the material of all creation. It was innate and a characteristic of all. Everything was holy.

We see this today with the reckless wielding of the word "holy." Some people still today seem to imply that everything is holy.

There is a restaurant, Holy Guacamole, which claims to have the ability to mash avocadoes in "heavenly" ways.

A friend of mine insists on saying "holy cow" every time he eats a hamburger.

There is an entire website devoted to the 353 "holy fill-in-the-blank" sayings of Robin in the 1960s *Batman* television show: "holy squirrel cage," "holy funny bone," "holy anagram," "holy armadillo," "holy unlikelihood," and "holy popcorn, Batman."[8]

Many people even shout "holy crap" to express their surprise—but what does this phrase express about holiness? How does our casual usage of "holy" shape our understanding of the term? Is there anything really set apart about "holy" when we use it in these ways?

When everything is holy, nothing is holy. These uses of the term "holy" are but a pale reflection of how God used it.

God being set apart from the world does not mean that God is absent from the world or that God is against the world. God is not just set apart from creation; God is set apart for creation as well. God is set apart for all that is good. God is set apart for recreating the good.

In the beginning God created. We might have messed it up pretty quickly, but God created and God still continues to recreate today. God is not willing to abandon creation. God is not willing to give up on creation. God is actively at work recreating in this world still. Matthew 19 tells us that God is working towards the "renewal of all things."[9] Colossians 1 talks about how God wants to "reconcile to himself all things."[10] Acts 3 is about "the time of universal restoration" for all of creation.[11]

So God is set apart from.

And God is set apart for.

But God is also set apart with.

God is set apart with all who share this vision. God is set apart with everyone who works towards that recreating of the good. God is set apart with those who choose to embrace their calling to be holy. Our Holy God, the God who is set apart, also sets us apart and calls us to be holy.

What does this look like?

***

Leviticus is the third book in the Bible. It is often referred to as the "holiness book" and it contains a lot of information about holiness and an overabundance of information about laws, rituals, and priests. Leviticus is a great book for us to look at, but is also typically the reason people stop reading the Bible if they are attempting to read it cover to cover. It can seem pretty strange and "out there" at times. I think we lose most folks somewhere around the point of Moses smearing blood on the right ear lobes, thumbs, and big toes of Aaron's descendants while throwing the remainder upon the altar.[12] But Leviticus really is a great book. It has a lot to teach us. And here is the short-and-sweet of Leviticus to help us to better understand "holy."

The book of Leviticus is 27 chapters long. The first section seems to deal primarily with regulations and rules regarding how we can approach God. We read about acceptable ways to approach God in fellowship, outside of fellowship, and through offerings. There is then a large part about the laws for a priest detailing the special rituals, processes, and accessories that one must have. Following this is another section dealing with the purity of the people. It takes us through list after list of what is clean and unclean, and how to make the unclean clean again.

This is all in the first section. This is all simply dealing with appropriate ways for us to approach our one, true Holy God. In chapter 17 of this book, however, we find a shift. Suddenly the goal of this holiness book is not simply how to be holy so that we can approach God, but how we can be holy and reflect God's holiness into the world.[13]

This is a major shift.

After chapter 17 in Leviticus we are less fixated on approaching our Holy God, and more attentive to reflecting God's holiness to the world.

The Israelites no longer believe God is just in the sanctuary. God's presence for them is no longer limited to a physical space. It opens the Israelites up to the idea that God can and does go beyond the tabernacle out into the world. It opens them up to the idea that we too are called to go beyond the sanctuary and out into the world.

For us, it reminds us why we go to church. You do not just go to church to see God, you go to church to remind yourself that God's presence can be felt and seen and shared everywhere.

In the rest of Leviticus we find some very practical ways to follow this shift. We see some of the most beautiful visions for humanity that were ever given. It describes how we can truly live together and love our neighbor. It teaches us about forgiveness even through economic measures—as in the Year of Jubilee. It contains what is possibly the clearest expression of our calling—to be holy.

The climactic moment in Leviticus is in Leviticus 19 verse 2. God is speaking with Moses on Mount Sinai as the Israelites are camped at the base of the mountain. God tells Moses: "Speak to all the congregation of the people of Israel and say to them: You shall be holy, for I the Lord your God am holy."[14]

In this verse we find an imperative and a declaration.

"You shall be holy" is an imperative. This is a command, a calling, an invitation. It is directed to Israel from God. "For I the Lord your God am holy" is a declaration. It is simply the statement of God's holiness. It is an explanation of who this God is that is directing Israel to be holy.

The imperative and the declaration match. There is a mirroring in the sentence structure. There is a reflection within the composition. There is a clarification of our calling.[15]

Our calling to be holy is issued by our Holy God. It is not left vague. It is not left uncertain. Our calling to be holy is our calling to reflect our Holy God. Just as there is intentional mirroring in the sentence structure, there is intentional mirroring in our reflecting of holiness. Our calling to be holy is not intrinsically related to morals or perfection or achievement—it is related to God. We do this by being set apart. We reflect our Holy God by being set apart *from* all that is not holy, *for* all that is holy, and *with* all who are holy.

To be holy is to reflect God's holiness.

One of my favorite songs is "Refiner's Fire" by Brian Doerksen. I first heard this song at a summer camp where I worked during college. It has a beautiful melody and devotional-feel to it. The chorus reads like this:

Refiner's fire,
my heart's one desire
is to be holy—

> set apart for You Lord.
> I choose to be holy—
> set apart for you my master,
> ready to do your will.[16]

I enjoyed it. I sang it. I played it on my guitar. But I did not really understand the lyrics for about another three years. I was leading a youth choir and we were singing this song. One of the parents was with us and asked us if anyone knew what a "refiner's fire" was.

I responded by saying, "Yeah, you all should really know what you're singing. Why don't you tell them about it?" But truthfully, I had no idea. #sillyyouthpastor

He told us.

A refiner's fire is used in the purification process for precious metals. The song begins with: "Purify my heart, let me be as gold…pure gold." The one working the metal places it in a blazing, hot fire. This fire is then used to purify the metal. It cleanses the metal from impurities. It eliminates what should not be there. Once the metal gets to this point, it is so hot and so pure that it looks like a mirror. It actually reflects the image of the metal worker.

That's what our calling to be holy is all about. It is about God working in us, through us, and on us. It is about God cleansing us. It is about clearly seeing our Holy God and reflecting God's holiness in this world.

***

When I was younger I went through a period of only wanting to wear "Christian" t-shirts. These were the t-shirts I got in my church, or at my summer bible camp, or from those franchise-Jesus catalogues that seem to just magically appear in all junior high youth rooms. I always wanted to wear them because I saw it as my job to wear these t-shirts. I thought of it as my work that only I could do. I had to wear those t-shirts because everyone I saw needed to see them. Because if I did not wear those shirts, how would people ever find out about Jesus?

I thought way too much of myself.

I thought way too little of God.

How arrogant it was to think that God could only work through me. How narcissistic it was to think that God could only speak to people through my t-shirts. How dare I limit God's actions to what I can do.

There is absolutely nothing wrong with wearing these kinds of t-shirts. I often still wear t-shirts like this. But no longer am I of the illusion that I must wear these t-shirts so that people will suddenly be granted the ability to see God. I am not the gatekeeper who gives access to God. God's voice in this world is not dependent on my fashion choices. God's presence is revealed in a lot better ways than my t-shirts.

We often fall into this trap. We think that we have to do something so that God is then able to do something. We think that God needs us to do it. We think that God is unable to accomplish in this world without us. We think that God is incapable without us. We think that God is powerless without us.

Think bigger—for our God is so much bigger than that.

God does not need us to accomplish anything. God's power is not limited to us. God's holiness is not limited to us. Our calling to be holy has very little to do with what God can accomplish in this world. God is at work all around us all the time. God does not need us to reflect God's holiness into this world. God can show up whenever, wherever, however. God is God, we are not.

But God calls us anyway. God invites us to be holy. God wants to work with us, in us, through us, among us.

Why?

God does not need us—we need God.

The mission of God does not need us—we need it.

When we embrace our calling to be holy, we not only participate in God's recreating the world but we participate in God's recreating of us. That is the best part of our calling. By accepting the invitation and living to reflect God's holiness in this world, we actually are the ones who change the most. We are the ones who experience the greatest transformation. We benefit. These benefits do not come as money, fame, or power—but as identity, belonging, and purpose.

Be holy. Listen to the yearning deep inside of you. Become who God is making you. Reflect God's holiness. In doing this you will discover who you are, where you belong, and why you are here.

set apart from…

find identity

chapter 4–lost

"Be not another, if you can be yourself."
—*Paracelsus*

"Do not be conformed to this world, but be transformed
by the renewing of your minds..."
—*Romans 12:2*

"To sacrifice what you are and to live without belief,
that is a fate more terrible than dying."
— *Joan of Arc*

When I was younger, I went with my mom and grandmother to a craft fair. It was one of those large downtown convention center craft fairs with booths, tents, and tables lining the walls and forming the aisles. It was basically a never-ending labyrinth of handmade quilts, crochet patterns, and smocked outfits for kids. #superboring

But then I saw it: the wooden train booth. It had hand-carved trains and tracks out to explore and entice. I am not sure if I ran to the booth or magically floated towards it, but this was the most exciting thing I had seen all day. To a four-year-old boy living in a pre-Thomas the Tank Engine world, this was heaven.

It was while I was attaching the engine cars to the cargo carts and maneuvering them through the town and trees and tunnels...that I had the realization. I turned to look for my mom—she was gone. I looked the other way for my grandmother—she was gone too. I remember feeling this overwhelming sense of panic set in. I remember the tears welling up. I remember the shakiness of my scream.

I was lost.

It only lasted about 30 seconds. My mom found me pretty quick. The length of time was minimal, but the memory remains intense.

Were you ever lost as a child?

Were you ever lost at a craft fair?

Do you still have nightmares about the knitting needles too?

There was another instance a couple of years later when our family went to a lake with some friends for a cookout. I am assuming all the parents coordinated this trip in some manner, because all the kids had bicycles and there was a paved path right by our pavilion.

I remember riding with the bicycle gang down the path until we were just about out of sight of our parents. I remember all the kids at that point deciding to turn around. I remember my sister insisting that I too should turn around. I remember wanting to go on. All the other kids went back. I did not. I kept going. By myself.

A couple of minutes into my solo journey, the magnitude of my solitude hit me. I was alone. I did not know where I was. I was lost…again. I remember sobbing on my bike as I slowly pedaled inch by inch down the path. I remember fleeing from the strangers at the next pavilion who kept asking if I was okay. I remember the sun beginning to set. And I remember how glad I was to see my dad when he chased me down. I was so happy to see him that I refused to let him put me down. I made him carry me and my bike all the way back to the pavilion. #superdad

What do you remember about being lost as a kid?

How did it make you feel?

When I share these stories about being lost, I always hear stories in return. It seems to be a rite of passage for all children. Perhaps our parents all decided to temporarily lose us in our younger years to teach us about being lost. Maybe it is a part of our initiation. Maybe it is a giant parental prank. But these are often the stories that we never forget. The details and the particulars might become a little fuzzy over time, but we all remember the feeling in that moment. We all remember what it felt like to be lost. We all remember that empty, hollow feeling of confusion and absence.

We can all remember it, but how many of us have experienced it lately?

I am not just talking about being physically lost. I am a self-confessing directionally challenged adult and I get lost all the time. If you are giving me directions, you should probably draw me a map. If I am late to a meeting, it is because I got turned around. If I do not show up to a party, it is not because I am rude, it is because I am lost.

I have been separated from my party at plenty of craft, career, and state fairs since the age of four, but did not scream at the top of my lungs the moment I realized it. I have ridden a bicycle alone since that cookout and somehow managed to not cry at all. I have had very similar "being lost" experiences, but have not always felt lost during them.

In a world of GPS and smart phones, we can be lost and never feel lost. We can be in a brand-new place in the middle of nowhere and have no clue about our surroundings, but we do not necessarily feel lost. We do not automatically feel that empty, hollow feeling of confusion and absence. Sometimes "being" and "feeling" are different. We can feel lost in very familiar places. We can feel lost without ever moving.

Being lost and feeling lost do not always go together.

So when was the last time you felt lost?

***

There is a memorable scene in the movie Anger Management. Adam Sandler plays the main character, Dave. Jack Nicholson plays the counselor who asks him the question, "Who are you?" Then Nicholson keeps interrupting as Sandler struggles to answer.[1]

Counselor: So Dave, tell us about yourself. Who are you?
Dave: Well, I am an executive assistant at a major pet products company.
Counselor: I don't want you to tell us what you do. I want you to tell us who you are.
Dave: All right. I'm a pretty good guy. I like playing tennis on occasion.
Counselor Also, not your hobbies, Dave. Just simple: tell us who you are.
Dave: I'm a nice, easygoing man.
Counselor: Dave, you're describing your personality. I want to know who you are.

Then Sandler's character, unable to manger his anger anymore, blurts out:

Dave: What do you want me to say? I mean, I'm sorry. I want to answer your question. I'm just not doing it right, I guess.

Why is this scene so memorable? It is a funny movie with great comedic acting, but the scene by itself is not all that impressive. This scene does not further the storyline. This scene does not reveal any new information. This scene did not even make me #LOL when I first watched it.

So what is so great about this scene?

This scene is so great because it connects you to Dave. It connects you to Sandler's character. This scene is in the movie to help you identify with him. That is its purpose.

Viewers are now drawn deeper into the movie. We identify with the narrative. We see ourselves in the story. We are now invested in the movie and the outcome. That is how they hook you. That is how they get to you keep watching. That is how they make it nearly impossible to step out of the theater for a popcorn refill and potty break. All good movies do this. All great stories do this. You have to be connected to a character to be interested in it. The story seems distant and unexciting if there is no bond or relationship between you and them.

So Dave expresses what we have all felt when faced with the raw, piercing question—"Who are you?" Panic. Fear. Uncertainty. A desire to answer, mixed with the inability to do so.

They are highlighting what we all know to be true. When push comes to shove, we have all struggled with this question: Who are you? Not your hobbies, pastimes, diversions, distractions, interests, or what you do to relax. Not your job, work, occupation, profession, career, or livelihood. Not your personality, character, nature, behavior, mood, temperament, disposition, or outlook. Not what you do. Not what you produce. Not how you act. Not how you want to be perceived. But who are you?

Who are you?

We want to be able to answer this question. We are just not always sure that we are doing it right.

Friedrich Schleiermacher—German theologian, philosopher, and biblical scholar who was alive at the turn of the nineteenth century—was known primarily for his work comparing and contrasting the traditional Protestant worldview with what came out of the Enlightenment. Schleiermacher was a deep thinker with deep questions who did a lot to help shape the progress of modern thought and the understanding of human identity.

There is a story often told about Schleiermacher. When he was getting up there in years, he enjoyed going on walks. One day he sat down on a park bench by himself to rest. Schleiermacher sat there a long time. He began to reflect on his life. He began to go deep into philosophical questions about who he was and why he was there. He began to probe his own identity. He became lost in these thoughts.

Just then, a police officer walked by that bench. Suspecting that Schleiermacher was a vagrant, the police officer shook him and asked, "Who are you?"

Schleiermacher then sadly looked up and replied, "I wish I knew."

Now Schleiermacher did not forget his name, where he lived, or what he was doing there that day. Schleiermacher was simply being honest about his search for identity and his struggles with his sense of self. And if we too are honest, we have all been lost in these thoughts before. We have all felt that empty, hollow feeling of confusion and absence while trying to figure out who we are.

This can be hard for us to acknowledge. Feeling lost comes with a stigma. We do not like to admit that we feel lost—because then we might have to ask for help. We do not want to think that we feel lost—because that would mean something might be wrong. We do not want to talk about feeling lost—because we fear that deep, down inside we might actually be lost.

It is scary stuff. To allow yourself to feel lost is to allow yourself to feel vulnerable. You surrender some control. You admit that you are not perfect. You give up the illusion of having it all together. Whether you are a child or an adult, feeling lost is terrifying. So we bury it. So we ignore it. So we pretend that we have it all together—until it all falls apart.

We have all felt lost. We all still feel lost from time to time. We all ponder our identity. We have all thought, "I wish I knew," while brooding over the question "who am I?"

Without our identity, we just feel lost.

***

Our identity is who we are. It is our essence. It is how we distinguish ourselves from the rest of the world. It is what sets us apart from everything else. Our identity is what makes us…us.

But far too often in life we sacrifice our identity.

A piece of string walks into a bar and the bartender immediately ask: "Are you a string?" The string replies, "Yes." So the bartender immediately kicks him out of the bar and shouts that they do not serve strings at that bar.

The string, slightly confused and frustrated, leaves the bar and returns just five minutes later to have the bartender once again ask: "Are you a string?" The string timidly responds, "Yeah." So the bartender kicks him out again and repeats that they will not serve strings at that bar.

The string, now irate, walks out of the bar and gets an idea. He ties himself in a knot, messes up his hair and walks back in. The bartender looks at him and asks, "Aren't you that string I've kicked out of here twice already?" The string looks straight at the bartender and says, "Nope, I'm a frayed knot"[2]

How often do we tie ourselves in knots because of other people?

How often do we try to appear to be someone else?

How often do we try to change who we are for others?

Far too often in life we sacrifice our identity.

My skeptical nature flared while I watched the film *Catch Me If You Can*. Frank Abagnale Jr. was made famous in this 2002 biographical film based on his life. Beginning at the age of 16, Abagnale became one of the most famous imposters ever. He began simply by setting up fake aliases to open and overdraw bank accounts, but he quickly moved on to bigger and riskier endeavors.

Abagnale first impersonated a Pan Am pilot. This allowed him to fly around the world, stay at select hotels, and eat at exotic restaurants all at the expense of Pan American World Airways. Abagnale then posed as a teaching assistant and actually taught a semester of sociology at Brigham Young University. Following this, Abagnale served as the chief resident pediatrician in a Georgia hospital for almost a year despite his lack of training or credentials. His last big hoax was being hired at a law firm as a certified attorney.

I did not believe that what I saw in the movie could actually happen in real life. So I researched it with the ever-reliable Wikipedia, and according to them it is all accurate. This all really happened despite the fact that nothing about who he appeared to be was real. He forged transcripts, copied degrees, and rented uniforms. Abagnale was always pretending to be someone or something other than himself.

We are not as good as Abagnale, but have you ever faked being someone who you were not?

How often do you impersonate someone else?

How often do you portray a character trait that is not your own?

How often do we pretend to be someone or something else?

Far too often in life we sacrifice our identity.

I still remember parts of a keynote speech delivered at a small Missouri camp in 1995. I was in middle school and was attending a weekend retreat there. I have no idea what the theme was, no recollection of the context, and no clue about the speaker's name, but I do remember the analogy that he used.

He asked us: "Are you a thermometer or thermostat?"[3] He was speaking to a room full of young adolescents who had no idea what he was talking about and did not really care to figure it out, but he continued anyway.

"Thermometers simply report the temperature of a room. They record the ideas and principles of popular opinion. They adapt to be consistent with what is around them. They are changed by their surroundings. Thermometers conform.

"Thermostats alter the temperature of a room. They set the temperature. They set the standard. They make the popular opinion. They change what is around them. They adapt their surroundings to be consistent with them. Thermostats transform."

This was something the entire group of preteens in the room could relate to. This is something we can all relate to. Do we change ourselves or others? Do we follow the norm or set the new standard? Do we imitate or invent? Do we follow or lead? Do we conform or transform?

How often are we thermometers?

How often are we thermostats?

How often do we conform ourselves?

How often do we change others?

Far too often in life we sacrifice our identity.

We are constantly changing. We are always altering ourselves. This is natural. This is part of our ever-awaking awareness and our ever-growing worldview. Things change. We change. This happens. This is not inherently bad, but it can be. Sometimes we change ourselves for the wrong reasons. Sometimes we are altered in detrimental ways. Sometimes we are thrown, shaped, and molded by someone who has no business sitting at our pottery wheel. We ignore a part of ourselves. We neglect aspects of our personhood. We abandon something central to who we are.

What happens when we take away our core? What happens when we eliminate our essence? What happens when we totally change who we are, pretend to be what we are not, and conform to what is around us? What happens when we sacrifice our identity?

We feel that empty, hollow feeling of confusion and absence.

We feel lost.

***

We sacrifice our identity. We change, pretend, and conform who we are.

Others assault our identity. They label, stereotype, and underestimate who we are.

The point of advertising is to sell. The way to do this is by relating to the customer, convincing them that they are deficient or lacking in some way, then showing them that the seller can correct or fulfill what they need. Advertisers try to tell you who you are. They try to tell you what is wrong with who you are. They try to tell you they can fix you. This is a pessimistic way of looking at it, and not all advertising is bad, but the objective is to sell you a new-and-improved-you and the life you could have.

Researchers estimate that people were exposed to approximately 500 advertisements a day in the 1970s. These ads were on television, radio, flyers, billboards, magazines, newspapers, and some were even painted onto the side of buildings. #oldschool

Advocacy groups were shocked and horrified at this. They were outraged when they realized how much energy and creativity went into persuading their purchasing decisions. They felt tricked, deceived, and used.

Yet today, researchers estimate that the amount of advertising in our world has drastically increased. They now estimate that we see or hear around 5,000 advertisements daily. Five thousand!! That is ten times the amount of just a few decades prior. That is ten times the amount that the previous generation was already bothered by.[4]

Stop and think.

How many advertisements have you experienced in the last hour?

How many advertisements are present in your life right now?

The average length of a half-hour television show is now down to 22 minutes because of commercials. That leaves less than 74 percent of the time allotted for the actual television show. Over a quarter of the time is spent trying to directly persuade you to buy cars, clothes, cologne, or some other "must-have." The length of some commercials has also shrunk from 30 seconds to 15 or even 10. This is so they can try to sell you on more types of cars, clothes, or cologne. You could easily see up to 30 commercials by watching television for just 30 minutes.

Television is not the only medium to up the ante. Electronic billboards display multiple campaigns as you drive by them. Newspapers and magazines are being read more and more on tablets and computers with pop-ups and periphery ads throughout the articles. You can download tons of free games, podcasts, and apps that flood you with blurbs, endorsements, and quick fixes.

All day, every day, we are overloaded with people trying to convince us of who we are and what we need. Advertisers in the U.S. alone spend a total of 149 billion dollars each year to do this—149 *billion*. Billion with a "b."[5]

And it works!! Advertisers do not misspend 149 billion dollars. They know what they are doing. I am in awe of how twisted and manipulative it can all be. I watch *Mad Men*. I know how it works.

How does advertising affect you?

How often do you think you are influenced by the 5,000 daily ads you encounter?

How much of who you are is wrapped up in who they say you are?

How much of your identity is up for sale?

We cannot and should not put all the blame on advertisers, though. We do this stuff to each other. We constantly feel the need to figure out who other people are, and we often do this with little to no information about them. We stereotype people. We typecast people. We pigeonhole people. We categorize people. We make premature assumptions about people. We form opinions about people before we even meet them. We label each other. We brand each other. We give each other secret nicknames.

We use this incomplete information, right or wrong, to define each other.

Now I am not saying that all advertisements are bad. I am also not saying that all labels are bad. Some are beneficial and might serve a good purpose, but they are not your identity.

The problem arrives when these things stop describing us and start defining us. Incomplete assumptions and marketing strategies should never be allowed to tell you who you are. We allow others to disassemble our identity every time we try to live into what others say we are. We never fully discover who we are if we are trying to figure out who they want us to be. We were not created to be split. We were not made to be partial. We were not created to be less than we are.

Our identity is who we are. It is not who others want us to be. It is not what the world tells us to be. It is who we are.

***

"Who am I?"

This is the question.

This is the question about our identity.

This is the question about our identity that we ask ourselves.

But what happens when someone else asks this question? What happens when Jesus asks this question? There is a moment in the gospels in which Jesus does ask this question. It comes in the midst of his ministry. Jesus has been teaching and preaching. Jesus was healing and helping. Then Jesus takes a break, turns to his disciples, and asks: "Who do people say that I am?"[6]

One thing I am pretty sure about when it comes to the Bible is that questions are always asked for our sake. Questions help us dig deeper. Questions force us to reflect on what is happening. Questions are not for God. God already knows the answer. God does not need our response. Questions from God are asked for our benefit.

When Jesus asks, "Who do people say that I am?" Jesus is taking a poll. Not for his benefit, but to get us and the disciples thinking. What does the world think of me? What are the labels they place upon me? What nicknames do I have? Who do they want me to be?

The disciples respond with what they have heard and what they have been told. Some say Jesus is the new John the Baptist, who just proclaims the way. Some say Jesus is the new Elijah, who simply serves as the precursor to the "day of the Lord."[7] Still others say Jesus is just one of the prophets, one of the many people who speak for God.

But this is not where Jesus leaves it. Jesus is not interested in what the world thinks of him. Jesus is drawing our attention to what others say, and then directly asking us what *we* say. Jesus follows with this second question: "But who do *you* say that I am?"[8]

This takes it to the next level. This takes it beyond the objective. This takes it beyond a simple reporting of what they had heard. This makes the conversation more intense and personal. Now the disciples have to stake a claim. They have to express who *they* think Jesus is. And Peter is the first to respond to Jesus' question. Peter plainly states, "You are the Messiah."[9]

So how do we figure out who we really are?

How do we discover our true identity?

How do become un-lost?

John Calvin—famous reformer of the church in the sixteenth century—repeatedly said that knowledge of God and knowledge of self are inextricably linked. The more you know about God, the more you know about yourself. The more you know about yourself, the more you know about God. "Without knowledge of self there is no knowledge of God... [W]ithout knowledge of God there is no knowledge of self."[10]

The more we discover who God is...the more we discover who we are.

The more we discover the identity of Jesus...the more we discover our own identity.

"You are the Messiah."[11] It is in this simple statement that Peter not only stakes a claim as to who Jesus is, but he claims who he (Peter) is as well. Wrapped up in this term "Messiah" is an illuminating glimpse of Peter's worldview. The Messiah is the anointed agent of God appointed by God to help God's chosen people. This Messiah is sent because this Messiah is needed. Peter's confession that Jesus is the Messiah is also his admission that Peter needs a Messiah.

The Messiah is the one who helps the people of God. The Messiah is the one who is to deliver us from the bonds of this world. The Messiah is one who is set apart to set us apart. And in defining the Messiah, we define ourselves. We are the ones who are being helped, we are the ones who are being delivered, and we are the ones who are being set apart.

If Jesus is the one we call Messiah, then we are the ones being changed.

If Jesus is the one we call Messiah, then we are the ones being set apart.

If Jesus is the one we call Messiah, then we are the ones called to be holy.

***

We are called to be set apart from the world, the common, the norm, the labels, the assumptions, the stereotypes. We are called to be set apart from all that is unholy, from all that is ordinary, from all that is common. We are called to be set apart from all of this so that we can be set apart to be who we are.

Deuteronomy 7 tells us: "For you are a people holy to the Lord your God; the Lord your God has chosen you out of all the peoples on earth to be his people, his treasured possession."[12] We are set apart from all this to be God's treasured possession, God's precious people—cherished, valued, loved.

First Corinthians 3 says: "God's temple is holy, and you are that temple."[13] We are set apart from all this to be God's temple. We are set apart from all this to be the place where God dwells in us, lives with us, and works through us for the benefit of all.

First Peter 2 invites us to, "Come to him, a living stone, though rejected by mortals yet chosen and precious in God's sight, and like living stones, let yourselves be built into a spiritual house, to be a holy priesthood."[14] We are set apart from all this to be a holy priesthood—the people of God living the mission of God with the power, support, and love of God.

When we choose to change, pretend, and conform who we truly are, how are we living as God's treasured possessions? Are we a holy priesthood reflecting God in this world, or are we ordinary individuals trying to blend in? Are we filled with the Holy Spirit serving as God's holy temple? Or are we filled with that empty, hollow feeling of confusion and absence as we idle in our lostness?

When we refuse to be who we are, we refuse our calling to be holy.

When we reject our identity, we reject our invitation to holiness.

Be holy.

Find identity.

chapter 5—beloved

*"Beloved, let us love one another, because love is from God;
everyone who loves is born of God and knows God."*
— *1 John 4:7*

*"Define yourself radically as one beloved by God. This is the true self. Every
other identity is illusion."*
— *Brennan Manning*

"Being the Beloved constitutes the core truth of our existence."
— *Henri Nouwen*

Actress Thandie Newton gave a TED talk a while back about growing into her identity.[1]

Thandie's mother is from Zimbabwe and her father is British. She spent some time growing up with her family in both of these places before she enrolled in London's Art Educational School at the age of 11. She studied dance there until a back injury prevented her from continuing. That is when she began to pursue acting. That is when she began to excel at acting. You might know her from movies such as *Mission Impossible 2* or *The Pursuit of Happyness* or even *Crash*.

In this TED talk, Thandie talked about her struggle with identity. Growing up in different places, experiencing various cultures, always feeling like an outsider, Thandie explained: "I was the black atheist kid in the all-white Catholic school run by nuns. I was an anomaly, and my self was rooting around for definition and trying to plug in." She was constantly wrestling with who she was.

This is part of why Thandie loved dancing and acting so much. It allowed her to take on a new role. It allowed her to pretend to be someone else while she figured out who she was. It gave her permission to temporarily

49

find her identity outside of herself. This eventually led her to discover where we can all find our true identity.

Toward the end of her talk, Thandie said: "The self's struggle for authenticity and definition will never end unless it's connected to its creator." She and I may have a very different way of viewing this world, but we do share this extremely important belief in common.

We will never fully know who we are unless we are connected to our Creator.

I could not agree more.

Our calling to be holy helps us find our identity. It does not help us in some vague, loose kind of way. It helps us directly and personally discover who we are by connecting us to our direct and personal God. The more we are connected to God, the more we are set apart from the distractions, the more we embrace holiness…the more we discover our identity.

This is because it is God who knows who we are.

This is because it is God who reveals who we are.

This is because it is God who loves who we are.

***

Jeremiah was a prophet called to speak to the Israelites during a hard period of their life. The nation of Israel split into two nations back in the tenth century B.C.E. The Northern Kingdom (Israel) was destroyed when the Assyrians invaded about 200 years after the split, and the Southern Kingdom (Judah) fell to the Babylonians about a century and a half after that. This period is called the time of the exile.

Families were split. People were displaced. Cities left in ruin. The temple destroyed.

The Israelites, in many ways, had lost their sense of identity. They were God's chosen people. They were given the promised land. They were the elect. They were special. They were holy. But then it all seemed to vanish. They felt as though they were none of those things anymore. Jeremiah was speaking to a people who no longer seemed to know who they were.

In the very beginning of his story, we hear the call of Jeremiah. God spoke to Jeremiah and said: "Before I formed you in the womb I knew you, and before you were born I consecrated you; I appointed you a prophet to the nations."[2]

God knew Jeremiah prebirth.

And God consecrated Jeremiah before he was born.

This means God made Jeremiah holy before he even entered this world.

God then appointed Jeremiah to go and tell the people. Go and tell the people that God hears them. Go and tell the people that God sees them. Go and tell the people that God calls them. Go and tell the people that God knows who they are even if they no longer know do.

Jeremiah saw these words from God as a message worth spreading. It is a message of hope. It is a message about identity. God can see us even when we cannot clearly see ourselves. God hears us in the midst of our ramblings and noise. God calls to us, even if we are still trying to figure out what a calling is. God knows us, even if we do not.

Matthew 10 states that God knows you so well that "even the hairs of your head are all counted."[3]

I find it reassuring to know that our God is an intimate God. God knows who I am. God knows my true identity. Not what I pretend to be. Not what I aspire to be. But the true, plain me. God knows me.

Think of all the people who *kind of* know you in this world.

Think of all the people who know *of* you.

Think of all the people who know *about* you.

The world is full of people who might know your name, but how many of them truly know you? How many of them know your hopes, dreams, or visions? How many of them know your fears, worries, and anxieties? How many of them know the extent of your passion? How many of them know what keeps you up at night? How many of them have counted the hairs on your head?

People do not typically know you as well as you think they do.

We do not let people get to know the true us very easily. We do not always want the world to know the true us. We often recognize and conceal aspects of ourselves. We see some of our blemishes, so we cover them up. We hide parts of us from the world around us.

This is not some devious scheme we invented; it is simply the way we function. Think of your Facebook page. Think of what you typically post on your Facebook page. Do your status updates reflect your whole life, or just the parts you want to share? Does your timeline record your failures as well as your successes? Have you ever untagged an unflattering photo? Is your "about you" section truly all-inclusive?

We project the best possible image of ourselves online because we are in control of this. This is not necessarily lying or deceitful, but it is by no means the whole truth either. This is what some call our "projected identity"—who we want the world to see us as. This is an identity that is only partially true, so this is an identity that is also partially false. This is an identity that we cannot live up to. This is an identity that is not real.

We are getting really good at projecting the identity we want in this world. We are getting so good at it that we sometimes start believing it. We start to buy into our own projected identity. We start to believe only certain parts of our own story. We start to believe what should be unbelievable.

I recently watched a documentary about the brains of serial killers, and their abnormal ability to separate and rationalize the gruesome things they do from who they think they are. #movienight #popcorn

Most serial killers are psychopaths, but a psychopath is not necessarily a serial killer. A psychopath is simply one who compartmentalizes his or her life. They understand their lives not as one whole unit, but as several distinct, separate parts. They do not see life as one continuous story, but as several distinct, detached episodes. This is what gives serial killers the ability to commit horrible atrocities and then go on with life as usual. They are psychopaths. They separate that chunk of life from the rest.

Neurologists say that psychopaths compartmentalize to rationalize. They excuse parts of their life because they separate them out. They assure themselves that their true self is different than who they might have been in those bad moments. They convince themselves that they are not a whole unit.

Neurologists also say that we are all psychopaths, just to varying degrees. We all do this to an extent. We all compartmentalize our lives. We separate our lives into work, play, family, and friends. We act differently in different situations.

Where on the psychopath-spectrum are you?

What is going on in your life that you choose to compartmentalize and ignore?

Is your life whole or segmented?

Living into our projected identity is living into a partial reality. A segmented story. An incomplete life. But our calling to be holy is a calling to wholeness.

In 1 Chronicles we read: "The people will be wholly at your command" as they built God's "holy house."[4] As the Israelites are undertaking the task of building the temple, they understand that this is not a side project. It is not some part-time job that requires part-time devotion. This is their life. This is their mission. They are called to be wholly invested in this holy project.

Because that is how it works. Our invitation to be holy does not just affect parts of our life. Our calling to be holy affects our whole self. When we embrace it, holiness does not simply become *a* story we live—but *the* story we live. The whole story. It shapes us. It molds us. It forms us into the whole, holy person that God created us to be. The person that God knows us to be.

God knows us to be us—even when we do not. God does not see us as partial, segmented, or incomplete. God sees all of us. God can see straight through our projected identity. God does not have to rely on tweets, posts, or notifications to discover who we are. God knows us.

And in a world in which even we get confused by our projected identities, it is good to know that Someone knows us.

***

When Jesus asks, "Who am I?" he also implies, "Who are you?"

When Jesus reveals who he is, he also reveals who we are.

In the fourth chapter of John we find an encounter between Jesus and a Samaritan woman. It is an odd encounter in the sense that Jesus is immediately breaking down social boundaries by speaking to a woman who also happens to be a Samaritan. Women were considered to be the lesser of the sexes back in those days, and Samaria was considered a less than desirable place for Israelites to be. Jesus once again was breaking the mold. Twice. #rebel

Jesus had been traveling from Judea back to Galilee. Samaria was in the middle. He decided to stop and rest at a well while his disciples were off foraging for food. This is where he first spoke to the woman. He asked for a drink of water.

Some witty banter is then exchanged. Some conversation of living water and eternal life is had. Then Jesus suddenly gets personal. He begins to reveal close, personal details about this Samaritan woman's life. He begins to tell her about herself. She then calls Jesus a prophet and asks him more questions. She states her belief that someone is coming. Someone great.

Someone that they call Messiah. Someone to proclaim and reveal all things.

Then Jesus said to her, "I am he."[5]

This is the first time Jesus spoke these words. This is the first time Jesus revealed who he was. This is a moment of raw, open honesty between an unknown outcast and the Savior of the world.

Two things happened in this encounter.

1. Jesus revealed his identity. Jesus told her who he was.
2. Jesus revealed her identity. Jesus told her who she was.

These two are connected. They are related. They are interrelated.

This is how we discover our identity. This is how we discover who we are. Knowledge of God and knowledge of self are forever linked. By opening her eyes to who he was, he opened her eyes to who she was. By revealing her true identity, he revealed his own. Barbara Brown Taylor—Episcopal priest, professor, and theologian—wrote this while reflecting on this passage: "The Messiah is the one in whose presence you know who you really are—the good and bad of it, the all of it, the hope in it."[6]

This is how it still happens today. You cannot encounter God and walk away unchanged. Transformation always happens in the presence of our Lord. A revelation is simply God giving us knowledge—God reaching into our lives and changing the way we view ourselves and our world.

So God knows who we are.

And God reveals who we are.

***

One of my favorite books is a children's book written by Max Lucado—best-selling author and wonderful preacher—that tells the story of the small wooden Wemmicks and the wood carver named Eli who made them.

There are a lot of obvious similarities between the Wemmicks and us. They spend a lot of time trying to identify and classify each other—except their labels are actually physical. They literally place stickers on each other to show how they feel about each other. The talented, strong, smart, pretty ones are most often given gold star stickers. The odd, clumsy, weak ones usually get gray dot stickers.

So all the Wemmicks are covered in stickers. Every day they get and give stickers. Every day they show the world what they think of each other. Every day the world sees what others think of them.

Punchinello is the main character in the book and he is covered in gray dot stickers. The world does not seem to think very much of him, so Punchinello does not think very much of himself.

One day Punchinello meets someone with no stickers. He had never seen a Wemmick with no stars or dots. So he asks her about her lack of stickers and she tells him to go see Eli, their maker. Confused and worried, Punchinello goes to see Eli. This is the conversation that then took place between Punchinello and his maker:

"Every day I've been hoping you'd come," Eli explained.

"I came because I met someone who had no marks."

"I know. She told me about you."

"Why don't the stickers stay on her?"

"Because she has decided that what I think is more important than what they think. The stickers only stick if you let them."

"What?"

"The stickers only stick if they matter to you. The more you trust my love, the less you care about the stickers."
"I'm not sure I understand."

"You will, but it will take time. You've got a lot of marks. For now, just come to see me every day and let me remind you how much I care… Remember, you are special because I made you. And I don't make mistakes."[7]

The closing scene of the book is Punchinello leaving the woodshop. As he starts to realize the significance of those words—and as the impact of what was just spoken to him sinks in for the first time—one of his stickers falls to the ground.

This is a story about finding your identity. Not in what everyone says you are, not in what you think you may or may not be, but in conversation with the only one truly qualified to tell us: the One who loves us, the One who cares for us, the One who created us.

Brennan Manning, a Franciscan priest, puts it this way: "Define yourself radically as one beloved by God. This is the true self. Every other identity is illusion."[8] You are created by God. You are loved by God. This is where you discover who you are. This is where you claim your identity.

This is nothing new. This is nothing unknown to us. Sometimes we just forget. Sometimes we overlook this simple truth. Sometimes we fail to recall the beginning of John 3:16: "For God so loved he world…" Sometimes we need a reminder.

A friend of mine once broke down in tears as he recited the beginning of Isaiah 43 by memory to an auditorium filled with hundreds at a youth conference. After talking about teen suicide rates and the dangers of ignored depression, he posed the question: "How much better would our world be if we all discovered our identity in these words?"

> But now thus says the Lord,
>   he who created you, O Jacob,
>   he who formed you, O Israel:
> Do not fear, for I have redeemed you;
>   I have called you by name, you are mine.
> When you pass through the waters, I will be with you;
>   and through the rivers, they shall not overwhelm you;
> when you walk through fire you shall not be burned
>   and the flame shall not consume you.
> For I am the Lord your God,
>   the Holy One of Israel, your Savior.
> I give Egypt as your ransom,
>   Ethiopia and Seba in exchange for you.
> Because you are precious in my sight,
>   and honored, and I love you."[9]

The Holy One who created you gives you your identity—and declares that you are precious, you are honored, you are loved.

Paul writes some similar words in the second chapter of Ephesians. Words of hope. Words of promise. Words to remind.

> But God, who is rich in mercy, out of the great love with which he loved us even when we were dead through our trespasses, made us alive together with Christ—by grace you have been saved… For we are what he has made us, created in Christ Jesus for good works, which God prepared beforehand to be our way of life."[10]

The God who created you gives you your identity—and in great love takes you from death to life.

God knows who you are, God reveals your true identity, and God loves you more than you can imagine.

***

We, in general, are bad at math.

Retail stores are figuring this out. They are now moving away from percentage-sales: "40 percent off," "one-third markdowns," "save half." They are more likely to use "dollar-off-sales" ($5 off a purchase of $50) or BOGO (buy-one-get-one free). This is not because it is better for them financially, but because we are bad at math. They say the average consumer can no longer do the percentage-math in their heads. They get confused. They lose count. They get irritable. They do not enjoy the experience. They do not come back. #epicfail

This is all because we, in general, are bad at math.

We are also bad at math because of the way we hear and receive information. Some information seems to be divided and reduced while some information seems to be multiplied and enlarged. People sometimes call this "critic's math."

Think about yourself and the information you receive from co-workers, peers, teachers, whoever. If you receive twenty compliments and one critique, what do you dwell on? If you are like me, you dwell on the one critique. What do you forget about? We instantly forget all about the twenty compliments.

If you are right 9 out of 10 times, which time lingers in your memory? If your kid gets all "A's" and one "C" on a report card, what do you typically focus on? Why do we dwell on the negative? Why are we consumed by what is wrong? What makes us unable to find the average or balance? What forces us to dwell on the lesser?

Our God is a personal God. Our God is not a distant, unknown, unknowing God. I know this to be true. God is always in the midst of this world speaking to us each and every day.

So why do I find it so hard to stop and listen sometimes?

Why do I feel the need to figure it all out myself?

Why do I feel like I need to keep going—constantly, endlessly, tirelessly?

I am much better at listening to what others in this world say about me. I constantly seek approval from individuals and groups. I care so much about their words and descriptions of myself. They drip compliments or drop complaints about me and I soak it all up as if it is the absolute and final truth about me, as if that is what defines who I am. Why do I listen to their puny puddles of feedback and ignore God's revealing flood of love and acceptance?

We were created in God's image. We were created from the dust of the earth and had the breath of life breathed into us for no other reason but to glorify and enjoy God forever. Jesus invites everyone he meets into a personal relationship with him—the outcasts, the sinners, the lepers, the men, the women, the children. Jesus cares about them all. The Holy Spirit works in and through and on and around us to continually recreate this world and reshape our worldview.

Maybe the problem is that we do not trust God. Maybe we do not fully know the extent of God's knowledge of us. Maybe we do not fully grasp the depth of God's love. Maybe this all-encompassing, overwhelming attention from our Creator is too much for us to handle.

Henri Nouwen—Catholic priest and author—calls this the problem of self-rejection.

> Over the years, I have come to realize that the greatest trap in our life is not success, popularity, or power, but self-rejection. Success, popularity, and power can indeed present a great temptation, but their seductive quality often comes from the way they are part of the much larger temptation to self-rejection.
>
> When we have come to believe in the voices that call us worthless and unlovable, then success, popularity, and power are easily perceived as attractive solutions. The real trap, however, is self-rejection.
>
> As soon as someone accuses me or criticizes me, as soon as I am rejected, left alone, or abandoned, I find myself thinking, "Well, that proves once again that I am a nobody... I am no good... I deserve to be pushed aside, forgotten, rejected, and abandoned."[11]

This is dangerous. Self-rejection is dangerous. These voices are dangerous. Not just because of what they say, but because of what they deny and obscure. Nouwen continues:

> Self-rejection is the greatest enemy of the spiritual life because it contradicts the sacred voice that calls us the "Beloved." Being the Beloved constitutes the core truth of our existence."[12]

When we self-reject, we discard the core truth of our identity as God's beloved.

***

Who we are is known, revealed, and loved by God.

God knows you. God knows all of you. God knows the whole you—even the secret parts that you keep and hide from yourself or others. And the amazing thing is that God still loves us. God loves all of us. God loves the whole of us. Romans 8 assures us that nothing in life or in death will ever be able to separate us from the love of God.[13]

But we all struggle with this from time to time. We all have issues with this overpowering, undeserved love. We doubt it. We ignore it. We misunderstand it. We place contingencies on it. We do this. But God does not.

Our calling to be holy does not come with strings attached. It is not trying to lure us in. We are already in. Colossians 3 states that we are "God's chosen ones, holy and beloved."[14] We do not have to be holy to get God's love. We get to be holy because we have God's love.

The choice is whether we live into it. Whether we live into our true identity or not. Whether we trust that God is the one who knows, loves, and reveals who we are or not. Whether we embrace this or not.

Be holy.

Embrace who you are.

chapter 6—identify

"My beloved is mine and I am his."
— *Song of Solomon 2:16*

"Your time is limited, so don't waste it living someone else's life."
— *Steve Jobs*

" 'Tis better to live your own life imperfectly than to imitate someone else's perfectly."
— *Elizabeth Gilbert*

Our invitation to be holy is just that—an invitation. It is not a prerequisite. It is not a qualification. It is not a forced restriction. It is an invitation.

I also refer to it as a "calling" to emphasize that it is God who directly and personally invites you—it is not a mass text message; it is a direct call. I believe God is calling us into a different way of life, a better way of life, a holy way of life. God calls us to this distinct life because it is a better life for us. It is more pleasant and more joy-filled than any life we could imagine on our own. God calls us to live a holy life because God knows it will be the best life for us.

In order for us to live this holy calling that God has invited us to, we must discover what it means to be set apart.

I wrote earlier that holiness is more than simply being set apart; it is being set apart in a specific and intentional way. To be holy is to be set apart from, with, and for. Holiness means that we are set apart *for* God and God's purposes in this world. It means we are set apart *with* all that is and all who embrace this invitation to holiness. And it also means that we are set apart *from* all that is unholy.

It is this last aspect of holiness—being set apart *from*—that helps us find our identity.

Our identity is what makes us…us. It is also what makes us…not them. Our identity makes us unique. It makes us distinctive. It makes us special. A basic definition of identity is "the qualities, beliefs, etc., that make a particular person or group different from others."[1]

So inherent with our calling to be holy is the invite to dive deeper into our identity. In discerning what you are set apart from, you discover more and more who you are.

So be holy.

Be set apart from.

Find identity.

***

Now we must be careful when we talk about being holy and being set-apart-from.

This can be misunderstood.

This has been misunderstood.

A few years ago there was a guy named David Koresh who misunderstood this. Koresh preached and proclaimed the need for a total separation, the elimination of outside influences, and a full devotion to what he said. He led a religious sect and built a compound in Waco, Texas, so his followers could completely detach themselves from the external world. In 1993, after some disturbing and upsetting reports about the abuse going on within that compound, they were confronted by law enforcement. The situation quickly took a turn from really bad to even worse. After a 51-day standoff filled with violent threats and eccentric demands and guns firing, the main building of the compound caught fire. Koresh, 54 other adults, and 28 children were killed in that fire.

This was a tragic end to a gross misunderstanding of what it means to be set-apart-from, and it was taken to the extreme by a deranged man masked by religious zeal. Unfortunately, it is not the only misunderstanding of this kind. In November of 1978, Jim Jones did something similar, leading to the mass murder/suicide of 914 in Jonestown, Guyana. Marshall Applewhite was also of the opinion that his followers in the Heaven's Gate cult needed to be totally devoid of the world's influence. In 1997, he organized the killing of his followers because of the arrival of a comet.

History is full of separatist movements gone wrong. The sects. The Nazis. The Crusades. They always take the invitation to be set-apart-from and modify it their minds to be set-apart-above. They then begin to imagine that they are above everyone else. They begin to elevate themselves. They begin think they are superior. And the scary part is that this shapes the way they view others. They begin to then look down on others. They begin to degrade others. They begin to reduce others to less-than-human status. These all are deviant deviations of what it means to be set-apart-from. These are all dangerous delusions that misinterpret our calling to be holy.

We are not set-apart-above anyone because we are holy.

We are set-apart-from everything that is not holy.

Note the difference.

But even this gets tricky. God calls us to be set apart from all that is unholy, but not to detach ourselves from the world in which we live. We are not to live our lives solely in a holy huddle. We are to remove all that is unholy from within us, but we are not necessarily to remove ourselves from the unholy around us.

In 1 Thessalonians 4 we read: "God did not call us to impurity but in holiness."[2] I think we can all agree that there is some impurity in this world. We have dirt, germs, and grime as well as abuse, slavery, and starvation. There are impurities all over this world. There are ugly messes stagnating and rotting around us. We are not called into this impurity so that we can dwell in it, we are called out of the impurity and we are called to help others escape it as well. There are many things in this world that we are called to be set-apart-from and stand against. But we cannot stand against them if we are nowhere near them. God is present and at work in this world renewing, restoring, and reconciling. God calls us to be present and active in that work.

In John 17 Jesus asks God to keep his followers "in the world" but "not of the world."[3] "In the world" means that we are supposed to be involved, invested, and present in our communities. But "not of the world" means that we are to remember who we are, where we come from, and why we are there.

I have heard it said that we are not to be isolated from the world, but insulated from it. We are not called to be isolated, secluded, remote, or totally removed. We are called to be insulated, protected, shielded, and set apart.

That is part of the reason God calls us to be holy. It insulates us. It buffers us. Not so that we can remove ourselves from the problems of this world, but so that we might have the audacity and boldness to face them. Not to leave and create a new kingdom elsewhere, but participate in God's recreating of this kingdom right here and now. Not to eliminate ourselves from the equation, but to exterminate the ugliness we see all around us. Not to run away from it, but to charge at it.

Jesus did this. Jesus was wholly holy and wholly invested in our world. Jesus did not back down from evil and he did not let it change who he was. Jesus was "holy, blameless, undefiled, separated from sinners," but at the same time was "a friend of tax collectors and sinners."[4]

So there is tension in our calling to be holy. Romans 12 says: "Do not be conformed to this world,"[5] but we are called to be in it. And when we do go out into this world, Deuteronomy 31 tells us: "Be strong and bold; have no fear or dread…because it is the Lord your God who goes with you."[6] There is something to be said for having enough confidence in your God, your calling, and yourself to go out into this world and to be the real you.

But what does this mean?

How do we live this out?

What are some practical ways I can continually remind myself of my calling to be holy and my true identity as one who is loved, revealed, and known by God?

I am so glad you asked. Please keep reading.

***

When I was a teenager I went through that awkward phase of life that we all go through. I was trying to discover myself. I tried to make my life make sense in my mind. I tried to embrace my uniqueness, my independence, my individuality. And while I admire my determination to do this, I now laugh at how foolishly I went about it.

I wanted so bad to figure out who I was that I began to imitate the cool, quirky individuals around me who seemed to know who they were. I remember begging my parents to buy me the same shoes my best friend had, the same hat my cousin had, the same jacket a kid down the street wore, and the same jeans shorts that everybody else already seemed to own. I got a skateboard even though I never learned to ride it. I collected POGS even though I never knew why. I owned a lot of slap bracelets even though I found them extremely annoying and they hurt my wrists. Kris-Kross even had me wearing my outfits inside out and backwards for about a week. #jump #jump

The ridiculous part of all of this is I actually thought I was being original by doing this! I truly thought I was becoming more myself by copying others. I believed I was more like me when I acted more like them.

Sometimes we spend so much time trying to be other people that we become what we are not. Oscar Wilde—nineteenth-century Irish writer and poet—once made the observation that "most people are other people. Their thoughts are someone else's opinions, their lives a mimicry, their passions a quotation."[7]

Do you really want to be someone you are not?

Do you honestly think God calls you to live as someone else?

We cannot find who we are in those we are not. We find our identity in the One who knows us and loves us, in the One who can tell us all about ourselves. There is nothing wrong with admiring the good and holy qualities in others. There is nothing wrong with trying to adopt some of those for yourself. But there is something definitely wrong when you simply become a mash-up of other people rather than yourself.

Part of owning our identity is owning our uniqueness. You are who God made you—different and distinct from everyone else. Just as every snowflake that falls has a unique pattern, every person God has made has a unique identity. When we fail to live our own unique life, we fail to live the life that God gave us.

There is no one else in this world quite like you. And the world needs you. So do not cheat the world out of your contribution by becoming someone that you are not. Own your uniqueness by shouting like the psalmist, loud and proud: "I praise you, for I am fearfully and wonderfully made."[8]

Be holy.

Embrace who you are.

Remain unique.

***

God not only made you to be you, but God also equipped you to be you.

I am a fan of Batman. Not in a stalker or rabid-collector-of-comics way, but I really like Batman. One of the main reasons I like Batman is because he is just an ordinary man. He does happen to be a millionaire with awesome athletic abilities, but he is still an ordinary human being without any superpowers. A radioactive spider did not bite him. A capsule did not bring him here from another planet. A meteor did not morph him into something else. Batman is a real, ordinary human.

The one thing that truly sets Batman apart is his utility belt. He wears this belt as he fights against evil and corruption in Gotham, and he always seems to have exactly what he needs when he needs it. If there is anything super about Batman, it is his choice of belts. #fashion

Batman has to walk out every night trusting that he has what he needs with him. Trusting that Alfred has put everything he might need in his belt, trusting that he will know what to use when the time comes, confident that he is equipped and ready.

What if we did the same?

What if we trusted that God has provided what we will need within us?

What if we walked out every day confident that we were equipped and ready?

Sometimes I think I am less than who I am. Sometimes I worry that my abilities are not good enough. I fret over whether or not God got it right when making me. I think, "If only God made me like that...," or, "If I would only be able to do this..." I have made plenty of excuses in my life for not living up to my full potential. But I am trying to quit.

God made us right. We are not mistakes. God made us who we are for a reason. God gave us the gifts, talents, abilities, and skills that we have for a reason. God calls us to use them. God wants us to embrace them. God wants us to develop and mature in them. God makes each of us different, special, and unique so that we can fulfill the different, special, and unique tasks within the mission of God in this world.

We not only need to trust that God made us to be us.

We also need to trust that God equipped us to be us.

Maya Angelou—American author and poet—once wrote, "I believe that every person is born with talent."[9] Do you believe this? Do you trust this? Do you know this to be true in your own life?

God has made us all with our own abilities. God has equipped us with talents. God has given us all gifts. First Timothy 4 tells us not to be wasteful: "Do not neglect the gift that is in you."[10] Romans 12 reminds us that we are uniquely equipped: "We have gifts that differ according to the grace given to us."[11] And 1 Peter 4 challenges us to make use of them: "Each one should use whatever gift he has received to serve others, faithfully administering God's grace in its various forms."[12]

When we live as who we are and do what we were created to do, amazing things happen. You will be surprised with what God will do through you. You find yourself excited to get up each and every day. You discover energy you never knew you had. You become contagious in that good way.

Trust how God made you. Trust how God equipped you.

Be holy.

Embrace who you are.

Use your gifts.

***

We are not journeying blindly in our quest for holiness. We have not been given an invitation with no directions. God fills our lives with guidance and advice, hints and suggestions for how we can be holy and find our identity. We just need to be open enough to receive them.

The church has always embraced the practice of baptism. And that is because throughout Christian history baptism has remained central in the Christian understanding of identity.

Baptism is a visible sign of an invisible grace. Christians have the symbol of the water, the promise of our God, and the faith of the believers. God claims us in baptism. God assures us in baptism. And somehow, in some way, knowledge of God and knowledge of self is revealed to us through it. Our relationship with our Creator is made tangible through baptism. Our holy covenant with the Holy One comes alive through the holy sacrament. This is what Christians believe about baptism.

What Christians believe about baptism is nice enough, but describing what we believe takes place in a baptism is kind of scary.

Stan Saunders—a scholar, a father, a former professor of mine—delivered a sermon about just this. He tried to remind everyone what baptism was really all about. He tried to emphasize that while baptism is a joyous, wonderful celebration it can also be mysterious, odd, and scary. His sermon was entitled "Death in the Family":

> While baptism is about new life and celebration, it is also about a death in the family. And I worry that when we baptize without making the reality of this death painfully clear, we are telling a version of the gospel story that has no cross in it. And that

just isn't the gospel. So, in case you are tempted to watch what happens here today and merely smile, I need to tell you what will really be going on here.

In a few minutes we are going to put my son Carson to death. And soon after that we hope that [he will be raised] again. In fact, if all goes according to plan, these events will happen so quickly that you might think the death didn't really take place. But don't be fooled. Carson is going to die today. [My wife and I] have come to believe that this is necessary because we no longer trust our capacities, as sinners living in a broken and distorted world, to raise him up…and to preserve his life from the powers of violence and death. We are convinced that his ongoing participation in this world will only corrupt and finally destroy him. So, we've decided to give him back to God."[13]

For the record, Carson did rise again. In fact, I believe that Carson is still doing quite well. But on that day, Carson died to who he was, he was made afresh, and he was given a new identity.

When Jesus was baptized, there was an overwhelming sense of God's close presence. Jesus went down to the Jordan River where John the Baptizer was dunking folks as he proclaimed the gospel. Jesus asked to be baptized. John dunked him. And immediately we are told that the heavens were torn open, the Spirit of God descended, and a voice boomed: "You are my Son, whom I love; with you I am well pleased."[14]

God said three things.

You are mine. In you I find delight. And I love you.

These words are uniquely expressed to Jesus at his baptism, but these are the words that seem to echo throughout every baptism. Through baptism God loudly proclaims, "You are mine, in you I find delight, and I love you."

There is a tradition at my church. Whenever the youth take a trip they are reminded of their baptismal identity with the simple phrase: "Remember who you are and whose you are." It is a perfect reminder that they are claimed by the One who calls them the beloved and delights in who they are.

This phrase actually became so popular that every graduating senior is now handed a framed mat with those words in calligraphy: "Remember who you are and whose you are." And it means so much to them that many of them hang it up in their college dorm rooms. It might be hanging next to a neon beer advertisement, but it is hanging up in their dorm rooms nonetheless.

This phrase and their baptismal identity were with them long before they knew me, and I hope they will remain in their minds long after they forget about me.

Be holy.

Remember who you are and whose you are.

Claim your baptism.

***

So God made you, equips you, claims you, enjoys you. But God also wants you to take the time to rest and reflect on what all of that means.

In the first two chapters of the Bible, we read that God created the world in six days. Then God created the sabbath on the seventh. #significantshift

The word "sabbath" comes from the Hebrew *shabbat*, which means "to cease."[91] So God was actively creating this world for six days and then God ceased on the sabbath. Why?

Scripture says, "Thus the heavens and the earth were finished, and all their multitude. And on the seventh day God finished the work that he had done, and he rested on the seventh day from all the work that he had done."[92] God stopped because God was finished for the time being. God worked hard creating this world in which we live and then immediately God rested hard, enjoying this world in which we live.

God observed the sabbath.

Then God told us to observe the sabbath as well.

#anothersignificantshift

Right in the middle of the Ten Commandments, we find the commandment about the sabbath. Some people refer to it as the bridge commandment, because it connects the first few commandments, which are primarily about God, to the last few commandments, which are mainly about us.

The Ten Commandments actually appear twice in scripture. The first time is in Exodus when God first reveals them to the Israelites, and they appear again in Deuteronomy in one of the five great speeches from the soon-to-be-departing Moses.

Exodus 20 says: "Remember the sabbath day, and keep it holy."[15] Deuteronomy 5 is a little stronger: "Observe the sabbath day and keep it holy, as the LORD your God commanded you."[16] But there, plain as day, we are officially told to observe and remember the sabbath and that the sabbath is connected to holiness. Why?

People told me growing up that I needed to go to church on Sundays because it was the sabbath and that was what you were supposed to do on the sabbath—worship God. While I still go to church on Sundays and I still see that as a good thing, I no longer believe that the sabbath is primarily about worship. Sabbath is about rest.

Think about it.

God did not worship on the first sabbath; God rested on the first sabbath. God had nothing to worship, but God did have something to rest from and enjoy. So if we strive to mirror our Holy God in our holy calling, then our sabbath has to be about rest.

Walter Brueggemann—the same Old Testament trivia champion from an earlier chapter—once inscribed: "Sabbath, in the first instance, is not about worship. It is about work stoppage. It is about withdrawal from the anxiety system of Pharaoh, the refusal to let one's life be defined by production and consumption and the endless pursuit of private well-being."[17]

The sabbath is to be kept holy because the sabbath reminds us who we are.

Sabbath reminds us that we are human *beings*, not human *doings*.

Sabbath reminds us that our value is not calculated from what we produce.

Sabbath reminds us that we are to enjoy life and not just endure life.

Sabbath reminds us that God is with us throughout the rest of the week.

Sabbath reminds us that we are loved for being just who we are.

The writer of Hebrews describes the sabbath as a welcoming of us into God's rest. In chapter 4 we read: "There remains, then, a Sabbath-rest for the people of God; for anyone who enters God's rest also rests from his own work, just as God did from his. Let us, therefore, make every effort to enter that rest."[18]

Part of the struggle to live into our calling and to be holy is to not get caught up in the rat race of life. To remember that your worth does not come from what you make or do. Nor does it come from how you act or pretend to be.

If we really believe our worth comes from the One who made us, the One who loves us, the One who intimately knows us—then maybe we should spend some time each week getting to know that One. And if we honestly believe that this is the same One who reveals our true identities to us, then we should probably accept the offer to sit and listen so that we can continually be reminded who we are.

How awesome is it that we have one day a week in which we are invited to rest with God and enjoy all of life?

Be holy.

Embrace who you are.

Keep the sabbath.

***

We live in a world in which it is easy to lose ourselves. We have all struggled with that empty, hollow feeling of confusion and absence, and we have all felt the piercing sting of solitude. At times we change, pretend, or conform who we are. At times others try to label, stereotype, and underestimate who we are.

Our struggle with identity is real.

But so is our God.

Our God is the one who truly knows us. Our God knows us so intimately that the hairs on our head have been counted. Our God is the one who loves us beyond reason, comprehension, and understanding. This is the God who reveals to us our identity. This is the God who can tell us all about ourselves.

And it is this God who calls us to be holy.

We are invited to live a life set apart from all that is unholy. To live a life that is beyond the common or usual or ordinary. To remember who we are and whose we are. To embrace our uniqueness. To embrace our gifts. To rest with God and claim our baptismal identity as the beloved. To be holy.

It is not always easy to live this way. We will still forget who we are from time to time. Old projected identities die hard. But our calling is one we can continue to grow into. Our invitation will never be retracted. It is worth pursuing.

Be holy.

Find identity.

set apart with…
find belonging

chapter 7—loneliness

"Turn to me and be gracious to me,
for I am lonely..."
— *Psalm 25:16*

"Loneliness is my least favorite thing about life.
The thing that I'm most worried about is just being alone
without anybody to care for or someone who will care for me."
— *Anne Hathaway*

"I don't want to be alone, I want to be left alone."
— *Audrey Hepburn*

Robert Putnam—a political scientist and a professor of public policy at both Harvard and the University of Manchester in England—has written several books, has done many speaking tours, and has informed us as a society that we are lonely.

A while back, Putnam wrote a book titled *Bowling Alone.* In writing this book he conducted surveys, calculated membership statistics, and directed personal interviews with nearly 500,000 people. What he found is that we as individuals have become more and more isolated from the world. We have increasingly detached ourselves from those around us. We are lonely.[1]

And not only are we lonely, but we are perpetuating a cycle of loneliness. We interact fewer times in talking and mingling with each other, and so we understand less about each other. We know less about those we network with and so we are not as concerned about who they are and what they want. We care less about people around us and so we lose our motivation to socialize with them.

We interact less with others, so we understand less about their lives, so we are apathetic about them.

We hang out infrequently, know little, and are concerned less.

We are even bowling alone. Putnam called his book *Bowling Alone* because more people in America are bowling than ever before, but they are not bowling together. Bowling leagues, parties, and socials are on the decline; meanwhile, the number of balls thrown and number of pins knocked down are on the incline. People are increasingly going to the bowling alley alone to bowl by themselves.

Putnam warns us of the inherent danger in this. By separating ourselves from our family, friends, and neighbors, we are unraveling the very fabric of our communities. This creates not just lonely individuals, but a lonely society.

Are we living in a nation full of lonely people?

Are we living in a lonely world?

***

I spent my summers in college working at a small camp and conference center. Each year we had staff training before the summer sessions would begin. Each year we had *the exact same* staff training before the summer sessions would begin. After hearing it all four times previously, I found myself falling asleep during most of the fifth.

But one year we had something new added into our staff training. We found on our agenda "Afternoon Sabbath." This was quickly noticed, highly speculated, and extremely mysterious. The entire summer staff began to pester the program director about this so-called Afternoon Sabbath, but she refused to reveal any clues about this elusive event. And so when the time finally arrived on our schedule, we were all eagerly waiting to hear what it was.

The program director told us that our Afternoon Sabbath was to be spent by ourselves. She said, "Go into the woods, alone, without anything."

We just stared at her.

Blank unknowing, unresponsive stares.

Imagining her lunacy—the woods? Alone? Without anything?

Quickly following the stares came the questions: "How long? How far away? How alone do we have to be? How come?" The questions were then quickly followed with rationalized complaints: "Can I take a book? I need to read this." "Can I take my iPod, it helps me relax." "Can we stay here? I don't have bug spray." "Can we go together? We need to work on tonight's worship."

To a group of highly social, extremely outgoing camp counselors, alone time seemed excruciating and wasteful. But the program director held strong and sent us all out alone for our Afternoon Sabbath. She simply asked that we try not to fall asleep (she stared at me when she said that, for some reason), reflect on the time we had together during staff training, and think about why we came to work this summer.

I remember dreading that afternoon as I walked out into the woods. But something happened out there. Something changed in me and in us out there. And so I also remember hating the walk back to the main campus five hours later when it was over.

I came back refreshed, invigorated, energized, and feeling more connected than ever before. It plugged me into our communal purpose. It super-charged me with a sense of our common identity. It gave me the time I needed to prepare myself for the work of the larger community. Who would have thought? Spending time by myself on that day actually helped me reflect on the fact that I was not alone.

Being alone does not automatically make you feel lonely.

Fast-forward two years in my life. I am living in Kenya. I am volunteering at a church in the city of Thika in the Makongeni parish doing some teaching, preaching, and learning. It was an amazing experience, but it terrified me at first.

I loved being in such a different context for ministry, but it was a tough transition for me. I had not traveled much. I had never gone overseas. I had never been immersed in a culture that primarily spoke another language. I got homesick quickly.

When I first arrived at the airport in Nairobi, I was late, it was dark, and I had no idea who was picking me up. Then the next few days were full of peculiar foods, odd travels, and strange customs—the only thing familiar was the clothes that I had been wearing since I left Atlanta the week before. #lostlugggagefail

And there were people…everywhere. Everywhere I went, there was a crowd. Everywhere I turned, people wanted to say hello. Every church I visited, they had a ceremony. Every school I attended, they held an assembly. I experienced some extreme hospitality while in Kenya and it overwhelmed me. It reminded me that I was different. It affirmed in my mind that I did not fully belong there. I was an outsider. I stuck out, stood out, and was worn out. In the midst of being surrounded by so many people, I felt so alone.

Being with people does not inevitably make you immune to loneliness.

Just as being lost and feeling lost are two separate issues, being alone and feeling alone are two separate issues.

***

Paul Tillich—German-born American existentialist, theologian, and philosopher—once reflected upon the wisdom of the English language. He wrote:

> Our language has wisely sensed the two sides of being alone. It has created the word *loneliness* to express the pain of being alone. And it has created the word *solitude* to express the glory of being alone."[2]

Being alone and feeling alone are two separate things. Being alone is what gives us time to reflect. Being by ourselves is what allows us to be us. Solitude can help us discover, imagine, or create amazing things in this world. But feeling alone is something altogether different. Loneliness can destroy our inspiration, motivation, and drive. Loneliness can be smothering.

Drew Barrymore—American-born American actress, screenwriter, and model—put it another way. She said:

> There's a tremendous difference between alone and lonely. You could be lonely in a group of people. I like being alone. I like eating by myself. I go home at night and just watch a movie or hang out with my dog. I have to exert myself and really say, "Oh God, I've got to see my friends" because I'm too content being by myself."[3]

There are monks who spend years in solitude and come back refreshed. There are teenagers who spend Friday night at home and think their lives are ending. There really is a tremendous difference between being alone and feeling alone.

Being alone is not necessarily a bad thing.

But feeling alone can be.

Feeling alone can convince us of a lie.

One of the great myths of our culture is that we are solitary creatures. We tend to be too individualistic. We often think in terms of ourselves first. We believe we can make life a solo journey. We repeatedly fail to see the interconnected web that shapes our world.

Edgar Allen Poe, the mysterious and often dark poet, had a difficult beginning to life. His father abandoned his family when Poe was not yet two years old. His mother passed away before he turned three. Poe was then raised by an unrelated couple who provided for his basic needs, but refused to formally adopt him into their family. Poe felt alone a lot of his life. You can tell this from much of what he wrote:

> From childhood's hour I have not been
> As others were; I have not seen
> As others saw; I could not bring
> My passions from a common spring.
> From the same source I have not taken
> My sorrow; I could not awaken
> My heart to joy at the same tone;
> And all I loved, I loved alone."[4]

When we feel all alone, we feel like no one understands.

When we feel all alone, we feel like no one notices.

When we feel all alone, we feel like no one cares.

We were not created to be on our own, detached, and secluded—but feeling alone can trick us into thinking that we are supposed to be alone, independent, and autonomous.

But the truth is that we are connected. The reality is that we do belong together. The good news is that we can rely on one another.

If you are feeling all alone, please read these next lines carefully. People do notice. People do care. People do understand…or at least there are people who care enough to try and understand. If you are feeling all alone, know that you are not. Your struggles are real. Your pain is actual. But you are not all alone.

You are never all alone.

So why do we feel alone?

***

I had recurring nightmares as a child. They were not the typical nightmares that kids have about the boogey man or knitting needles at a craft fair. They were scary in a different way. They were weirdly haunting.

I would dream that I was swimming in a pool or large body of water with friends and family. Suddenly I would sink to the bottom. The voices and noises would fade away. The others would become distant, blurry figures. It would get dark. It would become silent. I would keep sinking and was unable to move. I was stuck. I was still. I was alone.

Or I would dream that I was in an empty room with a puzzle. The room was bare and vacant and the puzzle was impossible. It would be something simple like putting a block into a hole, but the block was too big and the hole was too small. I would keep shouting that it was not possible. I yelled that I needed help with it. I would wait for a response and never get one. My cries would get more desperate and my isolation would feel more real.

I was lonely, even in my dreams.

It turns out that I had a habit of working through my issues as I slept when I was a child. I first began to sleepwalk after a close friend of the family passed away. And I first began to have these nightmares during a tough year at a new school with unfamiliar faces.

So as I slept at night I would face the issues that I did not face during the day. Dreams were how I dealt with my loneliness as a child, because I did not know how to cope with it at the time. I wrestled with it while I slept, because I did not work through it while awake.

It also turns out that not knowing how to deal with loneliness is common. We often do not know how to deal with feeling alone. We frequently fail to express our loneliness. We are not used to talking about it. We are not accustomed to expressing it.

Douglas Coupland—Canadian author and visual artist—primarily writes for young adults, but the themes in his novels are of universal appeal. One topic Coupland returns to in just about every story is loneliness. In the novel *Miss Wyoming* he writes this:

> Loneliness and the open discussion of loneliness is the most taboo subject in the world. Forget sex or politics or religion. Or even failure. Loneliness is what clears out a room… Loneliness is smothering…it stank of hopelessness."[5]

So we do not talk about loneliness. It is distasteful. It is unpleasant. It is not couth.

And the ironic twist is that not talking about your loneliness magnifies your loneliness. Our isolation is bad enough. Why do we amplify it by ignoring it? Why do we make the problem bigger by our failure to address it? Why do we think our current strategy of avoidance is working? Because loneliness is real. Loneliness is harsh. Loneliness is hard.

So far we have just hit on loneliness from an academic viewpoint. But it is not an academic issue; it is a personal issue. It is a very personal issue. We have all felt the painful sting of unsolicited solitude at some point in our lives. For the shut-in who cannot get out of her house. For the teenager with no parents around. For the mourning widow. For the struggling divorcee. Loneliness is tangible. Loneliness is personal.

Is this you?

Have you felt this?

Are you feeling this?

For others, loneliness might not have anything to do with a physical separation. Loneliness might be an emotional or spiritual withdrawal from the world. People talk about "crowded loneliness."

Now more than ever we are connected to the world around us. We have access to more people, more knowledge, more information than ever before. It is enough to make us feel overwhelmed. It can create a sense of crowdedness within our lives. There is so much that we cannot handle it. There is so much that we shut it out. We isolate ourselves from it. We barricade ourselves from it. We become lonely in the midst of a crowded existence. We feel alone among the multitudes.

Is this you?

Do you feel overwhelmed by life?

Do you feel alone even when you are with others?

We live in a culture that misunderstands loneliness, fails to identify it, and lacks in offering productive ways of expressing it. What hope do we have?

***

My wife and I are becoming excellent at selective ignorance.

For instance, we do not always see a pile of dirty dishes. Or we do not always hear our daughters when they begin shouting, "But I had it first!" And in the morning when our girls wake up, my wife and I do not always notice the flashing, vibrating, extremely loud child monitors next to our bed. It is our unstated rule that the first one of us to acknowledge the monitors is the one who must deal with the voices on the other end of them. So we wait. Try not to move. And hope to out-lazy each other until one of us gives up and gets up. (I almost always win.)

But perhaps our greatest feat of selective ignorance surrounds three cans of blue paint that we purchased for our bedroom walls a while back. We immediately took these paint cans home and put a blue sample splotch by the door to see what it looked like. We then promptly decided to wait on it, to think about it, and to paint it another day. Two years later…we hardly notice the blue splotch on our white wall anymore. It remains there, but the only time we think of it is when someone visits and asks, "Hey, why do you have a random patch of blue on your wall?" #abstractart

Selective ignorance is something my wife and I do extremely well.

It is actually something we all conveniently do quite well in life—we either become accustomed to something unpleasant or we chose to forget, discount, and distract ourselves from what is right in front of us. This is especially true when it comes to loneliness. We do not always know how to handle loneliness. We do not know how to deal with these feelings. So we often choose selective ignorance.

But selective ignorance has limits. Eventually the dishes need to be done, we must declare a ruling on who did in fact have the toy first, and one or both of us have to get out of bed. And when it comes to loneliness, selective ignorance also has limits. You come to a point in which you must either acknowledge your feelings or you must go to more extreme measures to distract from your feelings.

Studies show that people experiencing loneliness often search out pseudo-relationships. We turn to these things as replacements for real relationships. We turn to these things hoping that they somewhat fill the gaping hole of isolation we feel. But often these pseudo-relationships do more damage than good.

Some people turn to drugs, alcohol, or addictions. Some people become obsessed with work, production, or money. Some people turn to casual sex, affairs, or other emotionally dangerous behaviors.

None of these things are a true relationship. They are not designed to help with your loneliness. That is why they are "pseudo"—a Greek word meaning false, fraudulent, or pretending to be something they are not. Pseudo-relationships are not relationships at all. They are temporary distractions from our lasting problem of loneliness.

Now I am not saying that anyone who exhibits these pseudo-relationship behaviors is lonely, but I am saying that we can and do go to extreme lengths to deny our loneliness. We use these pseudo-relationships to avoid, to confuse, and to deflect the full force of feeling alone.

No matter how far we go to deny it, eventually our coping mechanisms malfunction. Our feelings resurface in unexpected or detrimental ways, and the ugly stench of loneliness is before us again.

***

My cousin used to work for Blizzard Entertainment. Blizzard is the company that produced World of Warcraft (WoW), a massively multiplayer online role-playing game. WoW is currently the most subscribed-to game of its kind and holds the Guinness World Record with over 12 million subscribers worldwide.[6] (I actually got a private tour of Blizzard's facility. It was awesome. They have a ping-pong room.)

In WoW, players create their own character avatars and chose a realm in which to place them. They immediately belong there. They immediately find their place. In this digital world, people are given quests, which connect them to the game's community and larger story. They sense that they are welcomed, needed, and useful.

Blizzard Entertainment has made millions by helping people feel like they belong within a larger narrative in which they can actively take part. People need a world like this. People need to feel like this. Somewhere they can find their place. Somewhere they can feel included. Somewhere they can be connected to others and a larger purpose. They find their place in a story bigger than themselves as well as discovering who they are meant to be and what they are meant to do.

This game does what we should be doing.

Helping people find their place.

Giving others a sense of belonging.

Inviting them on a new adventure.

F. Scott Fitzgerald once profoundly pronounced that this was the reason he wrote. He wrote to help people find themselves in something bigger than themselves and more meaningful than themselves. He wrote to help people find their place, to give others a sense of belonging, and to invite them on a new adventure. He wrote: "That is part of the beauty of all literature. You discover that your longings are universal longings, that you're not lonely and isolated from anyone. You belong."[7]

This is true of all literature.

This is especially true of Fitzgerald's work.

This is extremely true of scripture.

The Bible is our adventure. It maps out where we have been, it shows us where we can go, and it helps us find each other along the way. It is our gift from God: to remind us who we are, to guide us as we go, and to let us know that we belong.

In the twelfth chapter of 1 Corinthians, we find a beautiful image depicting our connected nature. It begins by simply taking about a body: "For just as the body is one and has many members, and all the members of the body, though many, are one body."[8]

A body is made up of all sorts of body parts: arms, legs, hands, and feet— as well as head, shoulders, knees, and toes. All these body parts make up the one body. They all go together. They all work together. They all are linked to each other. They all belong to the body. They all belong to each other.

This passage becomes a metaphor when we read the simple words: "… so it is with Christ."[9]

Just as a body is made up of many vital body parts, we all play a vital role in making up the body of Christ. Notice, it does not say you, individually, are the body of Christ. It says you, corporately, are the body of Christ. Because "the body does not consist of one member but of many."[10]

That means that we are all body parts in the body of Christ. I like to think of myself as the thumb or the aorta, although at times I feel like the ear lobe or the gall bladder—but we all are a part of it. We were all designed to be a part of it. We are all needed to be a part of it. We are all connected. We all belong.

We do not always act like we belong, however. We often forget that we are connected. We try to detach ourselves or we try to amputate others. Body parts seem to turn on fellow body parts—inflicting damage, hurt, and pain. Sadly, this is often true within the body of believers. Pain felt by one member—one part of the body—is not isolated. It is felt throughout the body. It is felt throughout the church. It is felt by the one we profess as Christ.

Sometimes we forget our own significance. We forget that we too are vital. And we become jealous of each other. We become envious of other parts.

> If the foot would say, "Because I am not a hand, I do not belong to the body," that would not make it any less a part of the body.

And if the ear would say, "Because I am not an eye, I do not belong to the body," that would not make it any less a part of the body. If the whole body were an eye, where would the hearing be? If the whole body were hearing, where would the sense of smell be?"[11]

Scripture describes a place where everyone can find their place. A place where we all belong to the body. A place where we all are connected within the body. A place where we are all essential. A place where we are all significant. A place where we are all needed. "If all were a single member, where would the body be?"[12] If we did not have each other, where would we each be?

***

To be holy is not to be set apart from everything.

To be holy is to be set apart from the unholy and set apart with the holy.

Set apart with all that is holy. Set apart with all who are holy. Set apart with one another. Set apart together. Set apart as members of the one body. Set apart with all the saints, with all that is consecrated, with all that is sanctified. We are set apart to be connected, to discover our interdependence, and to find belonging.

This is why we cannot view ourselves as disconnected. We cannot view ourselves as detached. We cannot view ourselves as isolated. For we are invited into the body to play vital roles in what God is doing in this world. In Ephesians 2 we find a portion of a letter written to express this same sentiment to the early Christians struggling with this notion of togetherness and community. It reads:

> So then you are no longer strangers and aliens, but you are citizens with the saints and also members of the household of God, built upon the foundation of the apostles and prophets, with Christ Jesus himself as the cornerstone. In him the whole structure is joined together and grows into a holy temple in the Lord; in whom you also are built together spiritually into a dwelling place for God.[13]

We are the saints. We are joined together. We are built together. We are called to grow into holiness together.

Be holy.

Find belonging.

chapter 8—communal

"When so many are lonely as seem to be lonely,
it would be inexcusably selfish to be lonely alone."
— *Tennessee Williams*

"[Y'all] shall be holy, for I the Lord your God am holy."
— *Leviticus 19:2*

"Communal well-being is central to human life."
— *Cat Stevens*

George Williams lived in nineteenth-century London. He was a farmer by trade, as he grew up in the country, but Williams migrated into the city and began working at a department store by the age of 22.

Williams noticed a lot of differences between country life and city life. Country life was marked by simplicity, sincerity, and a slower pace. It was marked by relationships, quality interactions, and a strong emphasis on community. (You can better understand this understanding of country life by listening to just about any country music song ever written.)

But city life was different. London was industrial, efficient, and corporate. Williams found city life to be rushed, complex, and superficial. He thought it offered very little in terms of community. Relationships seemed of little importance and everyone seemed to be solely watching out for their own interests. Williams did not like it.

Rather than complaining or ignoring what he saw as a problem, Williams decided to do something about it. He began to gather together with some other guys about his age. He would gather them for times of sharing, fellowship, prayer, and even Bible study.

Those who gathered with Williams became close friends. These close friends then began to invite more friends. Then the more friends began to invite even more friends. And this gathering eventually came to be known as the Young Men's Christian Association—the YMCA. The success of that group is directly linked to their reason for being—the need for community. Williams saw this. Others saw this. We see this still today. That is why the YMCA currently has a membership of around 58 million.[1]

Community is not the icing on the cake; it is the bread and butter of how we make it through life. Community is needed for us to survive. Community is needed for us to thrive. We were not made to be solitary creatures. We were not created alone and we have not been left alone and we have not been called alone.

We were created in community.

We were created for community.

We were called as a community.

Live communally.

***

In the beginning of our story, we find a beautiful, poetic depiction of creation.

Before God created the sabbath, God created the world. God spoke and the world came into being. And there is a refrain that repeats throughout creation: God created all of this, God looked at it, and God said "it was good."[2]

In the first three days God created light and separated it from the darkness; God put a dome in the midst of the waters to create the sky; and God gathered the waters together to create space for the dry land to appear.

God created all of this, God looked at it, and God said it was good.

In the second half of this creation story, God continued to create by filling what was made in the first half of creation. On day four, God has already made the light and now creates little lights and greater lights to fill the sky. On day five, God has already separated the sky from the water and now creates all the living creatures to fly and swim and multiply. On day six, God has already brought forth the dry land and now creates the cattle, creeping things, and wild animals on the earth.

God created all of this, God looked at it, and God said it was good.

We have got a lot of goodness inherent in creation. Some people believe this world is inherently evil, but I do not believe this is true. God repeatedly looks upon what was made and calls it good. So on day seven, on the sabbath, God simply celebrates and enjoys creation. God kicks back, rests, sips on a hurricane or a waterfall or whatever it is that God sips on and enjoys the work of creation. God enjoys the fruit of the labor. God enjoys the goodness of the world.

This is the mood of our narrative. This is the general sense after creation. It…is…all…good.

But it is short lived. Halfway through Genesis 2 we hear something different.

You see, God had created Adam—the *adamah* in Hebrew—the groundling. God created Adam to enjoy creation, but there was something not quite right. There was something off. There was something that prompted God for the first time in all of creation to say, "It is not good."[3]

The full sentence reads: "It is not good that the man should be alone."[4] Suddenly the disposition changes. The atmosphere shifts a little bit. It is not good that Adam is alone.

#gasp

Now I want you to realize something here. God is the main character in our story so far. God then creates this person and thus creates a second character. Two characters now exist—God and Adam. One plus one equals two.

So why does God say that Adam is alone? God is with Adam. God is for Adam. God is the one who knows who Adam is, reveals who Adam is, and loves who Adam is. God is intimately present with him and God is still the one who says, "It is not good that the man should be alone." [5]

Three chapters ago, we spent some time with the notion that we are created to be in relationship with our Creator: the One who made us, knows us, and loves us. This is part of our calling. This is definitely part of holiness—living a set-apart life. But we are also created to be in relationship with each other: the ones who did not create us, who may know little about us, and who might not even like us. This too is part of our invitation to be holy.

It is not enough to be one or the other. We must do both. We must be in both. This is a part of our DNA. We crave connection with our Creator and with each other. It is not an either-or. It is a both-and. Connected to God. Connected to each other.

Adam was already connected to God. Adam was already a part of that relationship with his Creator. But Adam was lonely until Eve came, because they were created in community. Before they were both created, it was incomplete. It was unfinished. Creation was not good again until they were both made. It was not good again until a community existed. They were created to be in community.

We are created to be in community.

***

Now this Genesis 2 passage is read at a lot of weddings. I know. I do a lot of weddings. I read this at a lot of weddings. #clergycliché

I read it and say something along the lines of: "Just as Adam was incomplete without Eve, so you are incomplete without each other. Just as they were created for each other, so you too were created for each other." #cheesyclergycliché

But at the point in the wedding service when I typically read this passage, let's be honest about what is really going on. The bride is worried about her dress being straight, the groom is trying not to pass out, the family is sobbing uncontrollably, and the rest of the congregation is watching the ring bearer tackle the flower girl.

They are not listening. They do not care what I am saying. As long as I do not cuss and I pronounce their names correctly, nobody will ever remember anything I say at a wedding service.

Because of this lack of attention, people do not typically walk away from weddings thinking: "The exegesis of that passage seemed incomplete," or, "I do not think they fully explored the depth of what happened in the garden due to the occasion of this day." Never once has a bride or groom asked to meet with me later that night to discuss the larger meta-narrative shift that takes place in Genesis 2.

But, in reality, something larger than this does happen.

This passage is not just about a relationship.

This passage is not just about a type of relationship.

This passage is about the creation of all relationships.

Before God created Eve, God went about the business of creating all the animals. God wanted Adam to have a helper. God wanted Adam to have a partner. We know this because God says: "I will make him a helper as his partner."[6] So God creates every animal of the field, every bird of the air, every living creature. God creates them all, but Adam is still not yet complete. We read on to see that "for the man there was not found a helper as his partner."[7]

Then God makes Adam fall asleep, takes one of his ribs, and from it forms Eve. Adam awakes, takes one look at Eve, and declares, "This at last is bone of my bones and flesh of my flesh."[8] As if to say: "This is the one. This is my helper. This is my partner."

I still use this passage in weddings because it has something wonderful to say in those moments. It contains an attractive appeal for a wedding and the romantic relationship that the bride and groom are entering into. But we cannot limit the Bible to certain moments of relevance. This passage speaks to us not just during a wedding service and not just in romantic relationships, but throughout our daily lives and in all of our relationships.

These words, "helper" and "partner," describe a relationship that goes beyond a marriage. While I hope these things are present in your marriage if you are married, these words describe a way of interacting with everyone in your life and not just your spouse. This "partner" will be on the same team with the same goals with the same purpose as you. This "helper" will assist and support and care and love you. These words describe a relationship that goes beyond just romance. These words describe a relationship that goes beyond one type of relationship.

Adam and Eve were not only created in community, they were created for community. They were created for each other. They were created to support, nurture, uphold, and strengthen each other. They were made to help, assist, benefit, and partner with each other.

And we know that this is not limited to just their relationship, because we see these themes throughout scripture.

Second Corinthians 7 tells us that we are to always keep the interests of the community in our thoughts and minds and lives no matter what we do or what happens to us: "You are in our hearts, to die together and to live together."[9] First Peter 3 tells us that in order to make it in this world we must "have unity of spirit, sympathy, love for one another, a tender heart, and a humble mind."[10] Then Psalm 133 reminds us "How very good and pleasant it is when kindred live together in unity!"[11]

We were created together to be together—to help, to partner, to serve, to love, to care, to cultivate, and to grow each other in holiness. It is not enough to simply say we were created in community. We are called to remain in community and be for the community.

Perhaps Hebrews 3 says it best—we are to be "holy partners in a heavenly calling"[12]

Holy partners.

Our heavenly calling.

We are created in community and for community.

***

I have recently embraced the word "y'all."

In the South, they take full advantage of "y'all." They use it in their everyday language. I grew up in the Midwest. We did not use this word. We would not have even known of this word except for the occasional Western movie that would appear on our television sets. For those of you from similar parts of the country who are still very confused about all of this, "y'all" is a contraction meaning "you all."

It has taken me a while, being an import to the Southern region, but I have finally come around to the word. It is actually very functional. It clears up the distinction between the singular "you" and the plural "you." When talking with groups, it saves time. When talking with Southern groups, it gives you street cred.

Our calling to be holy is a plural calling.

It is not just for you or for me.

It is for all of us.

The "you" in the Bible is almost always a plural "y'all" when it comes to our invitation to be holy.

In the Old Testament, Israel as a whole nation is continually called to be holy. In Exodus, the second book of the Bible, we read: "but you shall be for me a priestly kingdom and a holy nation. These are the words that you shall speak to the Israelites."[13] It does not say "these are the words for that one girl" or "these are the words just for you, Moses." The invitation to holiness is extended to the entire nation.

In Joel it says, "So you shall know that I, the LORD your God, dwell in Zion, my holy mountain. And Jerusalem shall be holy."[14] Jerusalem is not the name of an individual, but of the group.

Isaiah 62 proclaims, "They shall be called, 'The Holy People, The Redeemed of the LORD.'"[15] and Deuteronomy repeatedly says "for you are a people holy to the Lord your God."[16] This is not issued to individuals. This is not given to a singular you or me. This calling is not just for a person, but for a people.

And in the New Testament, Jesus does not shrink this invitation but expands it. He takes the holiness calling of the Israelites and extends it. Paul says, "There is no longer Jew or Greek, there is no longer slave or free, there is no longer male and female; for all of you are one in Christ Jesus."[17] So the "y'all" has been enlarged now to include all of us who choose to listen and follow this Jesus fellow.

First Peter 2—like the many parts of the one body metaphor—compares us to the many stones of the one house being built into what is holy. "Like living stones, let yourselves be built into a spiritual house, to be a holy priesthood, to offer spiritual sacrifices acceptable to God through Jesus Christ."[18] We are built together as a spiritual house. We are all connected to each other as a priesthood. We all belong to each other as we strive to be holy.

Ephesians 5 describes God's desire "to present the church to himself in splendor, without a spot or wrinkle or anything of the kind—yes, so that she may be holy and without blemish."[19] The whole church. All of us. Everybody.

So the scriptural command to "be holy" clearly has an understood "y'all" at the beginning of it.

That is why it is so crucial to see our calling to holiness as not just about who you are, but who *we* are. The invitation is not just about our connection to our Creator, but also to each other. It not only helps us find identity, but it helps us find belonging as well.

Be holy.

All of y'all.

All of us.

***

There are many times in my life, however, when I have wished that we were not created in and for community. There have been moments in which I think I would have preferred a solo calling. People can be difficult. Relationships can be tough. Community can be hard.

Arguments abound.

Bickering unceasing.

Anger bubbling up.

Loss breaking us down.

But we are called and created in and for community, imperfect though it may be.

God tells us that "it is not good"[20] for us to be alone, but God does not promise that living in community will be easy. Adam and Eve had their own problems, but their sons had more.

Anger is first mentioned in Genesis 4. Initially, Adam and Eve had two sons. Cain was the oldest and was the one who "worked the soil."[21] Abel was the youngest and was the one who "kept flocks."[22] In the course of time and when it was appropriate, both Cain and Abel would bring an offering to the Lord.

Cain would bring produce that came from the ground, from the soil, from the dirt.

Abel would bring the meat and fat from some of the best in his flocks.

Now we do not exactly know why, but God seemed to like what Abel brought better than what Cain brought. Maybe Cain brought some of his old, moldy vegetables instead of his best. Maybe Abel knew just how God liked the steaks to be prepared. But for some reason God seemed to like what Abel offered better than what Cain offered.

The text tells us that Cain was "very angry" because of this and his anger led him to attack and kill his brother. #possibleoverreaction

So very quickly after we learn that we were created to be in and for community, we find out that it is not always going to be easy to live with each other.

Anger, jealously, bitterness, and envy exist in all groups.

Pain, hurt, sadness, and frustration exist in all communities.

But so do joy, happiness, peace, and pleasure.

Not too long ago a young mother in our community found out she had stage III ovarian cancer. Hearts sank. Tears flowed. Community responded.

People began to show up at the hospital where she was diagnosed. There were too many to see her and she was not up for any visitors, but they gathered anyway. People started talking about ways to show their love and support. People started organizing meals. People started helping with the home. People started to pray.

As a visual representation of this, one night hundreds of people gathered outside of the hospital and lit candles. She was able to walk to the window. She was able to see all of them. She was able to feel the warm glow of her community. Nothing about that evening was easy for anyone, but glimpses of God's grace and peace were present in and among and through and with God's community that night.

Our calling to be holy is a communal calling, and what Ephesians 4 encourages us to do is "lead a life worthy of the calling to which you have been called" and then emphasizes that we do this "with all humility and gentleness, with patience, bearing with one another in love, making every effort to maintain the unity."[23]

Living in community takes effort. It is not easy. It will not ever be easy. But we are called to it. We are called to be in and for community—in the hurt and the joy of it, in the fear and the hope of it, in the better and the worse of it. We are asked to make every effort to maintain the unity of it. And we are invited to go on this journey of holiness together.

Live communally.

***

I have heard some beautiful, poetic descriptions of what will happen to us at the end of this life. Most of them involve a journey of some kind, normally towards a light or a staircase or a tunnel, and it involves a personal greeting or welcome of some kind. One of my favorites is that you will get to sit down with God and tell your story. God will remind you of the parts you have forgotten, cry with you during the sad moments, and laugh hysterically with you at the funny times. Then God will look you in your eyes and say: "good story, thanks for sharing it with me."[24]

I see nothing wrong with imagining things this way. I often like to sit and think about my story and how I would tell it to God. But I do want to caution against thinking about this all only as a solo journey.

Just as the first couple of chapters in the Bible paint a poetic picture of how it all came to be, the last couple of chapters in the Bible paint a poetic picture of what it will all come to be. Revelation 21 gives us a hopeful vision of the future. A communal vision for the future.

> Then I saw a new heaven and a new earth; for the first heaven and the first earth had passed away, and the sea was no more.

And I saw the holy city, the new Jerusalem, coming down out of
heaven from God, prepared as a bride adorned for her husband.[25]

In the end there is a holy city, a holy community. That is the picture given
to us in scripture. That is the image of what lasts. When we see the end
of our life as a solo journey, we start to see all of life as a solo journey as
well. And it is not. Life is to be lived together. Life is to be shared. Life is
to be communal.

We are called as a community.

Our calling to be holy is a communal calling.

We are created to be in community. We are made with others. We are
made as relational creatures. We are told that it is not good for us to be
alone. We are told that it is not good for us to live in isolation. We are to
be in relationships. We are created to be connected to one another.

We are created for community. We are created to help each other. We
are created to be partners with each other. We are created to love our
neighbor. We are made to support and nurture and care for one another.
We should respect and honor and value each other.

Living in community is not always an easy life, but it is a richer, fuller way
to experience life. We are called to be together and respond together as
we encounter our Holy God.

Be holy.

Live communally.

chapter 9—connect

"We are what we are."
— *Ke$ha*

"Peace be to the whole community"
— *Ephesians 6:23*

*"We allow our ignorance to prevail upon us and make us think
we can survive alone, alone in patches, alone in groups, alone in races,
even alone in genders."*
— *Maya Angelou*

We are called to be in community and for community.

We are called to be holy.

This is a calling that invites us to live a life that is "set apart with": with all the saints, with all that is consecrated, with all that is sanctified, with all that is holy. To be set apart as a holy community with one another.

Through embracing this calling to be set apart with, we can find belonging. By realizing that we are set apart with, we realize that we are not alone. We are not solitary creatures. We are not isolated. We do have others with us on this journey. This is a communal invitation. We are called to do the hard work of building and maintaining relationships and community— where we belong.

Belonging gives us an intimate connection with those around us. It allows us to feel close. It allows us to feel near. Belonging is what keeps us invested in and with others. Belonging is what helps us relate and bond with them. A shared sense of belonging is what unites.

Knowing that we are not called alone and knowing that we are communally invited to be set apart, we know that we have a holy community built in. The more you dive into your calling, the deeper you get into your community, the more you discover that you belong.

So be holy.

Be set apart with.

Find belonging.

***

Stanley Hauerwas—theologian, ethicist, and public intellectual—once wrote: "Saints cannot exist without a community, as they require, like all of us, nurturance by a people who, while often unfaithful, preserve the habits necessary to learn the story of God."[1] In other words, you cannot be a holy person without having a holy people. You cannot live a holy life alone. You need that holy community.

People are hungry for truth. We crave authenticity. We seek what is genuine, pure, and real. We want holiness. We want God. We want a community where we can question, ask, and belong. We want all these things and we need others who want all these things as well—we want church, we need church.

I was born, baptized, raised, confirmed, married, and ordained within the church. I serve as a teaching pastor of a church congregation. I took an oath to remain active within that body of believers. I pledged to serve God and the people through the church with energy, intelligence, imagination, and love for the rest of my life.

I am admittedly biased.

I love the church. I love the counter-cultural idea of people getting together week after week to worship Someone other than themselves. I love the radical notion of gathering to remind ourselves that we are not the center of the universe. I love the potlucks. I love the children's Christmas programs. I love the community I have found in the church. I love the sense of belonging I feel when I walk through the stained-glass doors.

That is why it breaks my heart to see people giving up on the church. I realize that my experience has not been the experience of everyone else. I know that some have not experienced a loving, grace-filled attitude from the church in the past. I recognize that some no longer feel welcome in a church. I lament that this is the case. And if this is you, I am sorry. I do not know exactly what happened, I do not know what was said, I do not know how you were treated, but I do know that the church sometimes forgets that it is called to be the church—and for that, I apologize.

The church is not perfect.

The church is full of flawed, messed up, inadequate individuals. We have hypocrites. We have frauds. We have phonies. We have charlatans. We have grumps. We have pessimists. We have bitterness. We have resentments. We have liars. We have haters. We have people who have done horrible, detestable things.

These things all exist in the church, because they all exist in the world. Every coffee shop, school, work place, government, fraternity, and civic organization contain these people as well. The church is a human institution. This means the church is limited in many ways by its mere humanness. The church is not perfect.

But the church is not called to be perfect. The church is called to be holy.

The church made up of regular human beings will never be perfect. But the church as the embodiment of our living, active God is holy. So the church is really both—imperfect and holy. And the church reminds us that we too are both—imperfect and holy. This means the human aspect of church needs some grace, and the divinely inspired aspect of church can continue to offer us God's mercy.

While I am not telling you that you have to go to church, I am telling you that you should expand your notion of what church is. The church is not just the pastor you disagreed with. The church is not just the deacon who yelled at you. The church is not just an angry, bigoted mob that aims to offend you. The church is so much more than that.

The church is so much more than any of those people.

The church is so much more than any congregation.

The church is so much more than any denomination.

The church is so much more than any movement.

The church is so much more than any doctrine, dogma, or creed.

The church is so much more than any of this.

The church is simply a community of saints—a gathering of people who are seriously striving to be holy—who accept this invitation to a set-apart life and who struggle to live into this calling together. This is an easy place to belong. This is a wonderful place to belong. Church might not always look like what you expect, but it will always be there for you. You are never alone on your faith journey. You always have company.

This is church.

Be holy.

Find church.

***

We are not flawless when it comes to living in community with each other. We mess up. We screw up. We hurt each other. We often offend each other. We neglect the needs of those closest to us while ignoring their feelings, opinions, and thoughts. And this all takes place day in and day out, over and over again.

So what do we do with this?

How do we deal with failures and disappointments?

In Matthew 18 we hear a story in which Peter—a disciple and leader in the early church who was referred to as "The Rock"—approached Jesus about this. He wanted to know what we do when mistakes or conflicts occur within a community. He wanted advice on how we should continue to live together. He wanted to know about forgiveness.

"Then Peter came to Jesus and asked, 'Lord, how many times shall I forgive my brother when he sins against me? Up to seven times?' Jesus answered, 'I tell you, not seven times, but seventy-seven times.'"[2]

Back in the day there were a number of rabbis who ran around teaching that there was a set amount of times that you had to forgive someone. They would set a number and say you did not have to forgive another person more than that many times. This seemed like a fair idea to most people. It seemed rational and easy to calculate. So it created a system. A system in which people would keep checklists referencing how many times someone had offended them.

Do you have a checklist?

Who is on it?

Am I on it?

Jesus' response to Peter was an odd one. He did not give him a regular number that a lot of the other rabbis were throwing out: two, or three, or even seven times (the number of completion). No, Jesus made it a little more difficult than that. His response was, "[N]ot seven times, but seventy-seven times.'"[3]

And even the number Jesus uses is complicated and vague. Biblical scholars comment on the elusiveness of that number in the original Greek. It could mean 77 times or 7 multiplied by 70 times. Who could actually keep track of 77 times? Who would actually keep track of 490 times?

Jesus is telling us to simply forgive, over and over again, without keeping track, without being bound to a checklist, or a system, and to let it all go.

But notice that Jesus is not telling us to "forgive and forget." There is a difference. There is a huge difference. Jesus does not call us to be doormats for people to walk all over. Jesus does not ask us to be punching bags for people to take their anger issues out on. You can forgive someone without forgetting and without putting yourself back into the same situation to be hurt again. There are many situations in life in which forgiveness is vital for your own personal health, but forgetting what happened and returning to allow it again would be very dumb and very dangerous. Please do not ever let anyone tell you that forgiveness and forgetting are the same thing. Predatory behaviors and abuse often happen under this misguided perception. You are called to forgive, but sometimes you are also called to remember.

And Jesus is serious about this forgiveness stuff. Why?

Jesus is so adamant about forgiveness because Jesus is so adamant about us living life to its fullest. How many of us are checklist forgivers? How many of us keep track—officially or unofficially? It is exhausting counting all the wrongs, calculating the offenses, listing the transgressions, is it not?

Forgiveness is about letting all of this go. Forgiveness is about freeing ourselves from the checklist. Forgiveness is liberation from retaliation. Forgiveness is about the release of ugly feelings. Forgiveness is about living your life rather than reliving others' mistakes. Forgiveness is about releasing yourself from the unnecessary cycle of vengeance. Forgiveness is often more about the forgiver than it is about the forgiven.

Forgiveness is about removing the control that they have on your life.

Forgiveness is about moving past the hurt, pain, and actions of others and back into your own life.

Nelson Mandela—activist, politician, and Nobel Peace Prize recipient—spent his life fighting oppression. He grew up in a highly colonized and highly impoverished South Africa. Many of the problems that existed in his life and country were due to the apartheid system of his government. Mandela decided to do something about the mandated segregation of South Africans. Mandela did not want that to be the world they lived in. After joining some resistance movements and providing leadership for nonviolent protests, he was arrested and placed in jail. Mandela remained there for twenty-seven years.

When he was finally released in 1990 and people were looking to him for a rally cry or battle charge, Mandela is reported to have said: "Forgiveness liberates the soul. It removes fear. That is why it is such a powerful weapon."[4]

Mandela went on to serve as South Africa's first democratically elected president from 1994 to 1999. He was able to be the instigator of change that his country needed—but it did not come through revenge or retribution or retaliation; it came through forgiveness.

Be holy.

Learn to forgive.

Be free.

***

People often confuse forgiveness with reconciliation.

Forgiveness is about letting go. Forgiveness is about being free.

Reconciliation is about coming back. Reconciliation is about being reunited.

Reconciliation involves action from more than one person. It involves two or more parties getting back to a state that previously existed. (This is where forgetting sometimes comes in handy.) This is when two or more people—both embracing the power of forgiveness—want to enter back into relationship with one another. They freely choose to return to each other. They so desire to rebuild their community.

At the beginning of Luke 15 we find Jesus in the midst of his ministry—sharing the good news, speaking the truth, and making the religious authorizes uncomfortable. The text reports: "He told them this parable."[5] Take notice that Luke uses the word "parable" in the singular sense, but immediately following we find three stories about God's grace.

The first two stories develop a pattern of something lost, someone seeking, something found, everyone rejoicing. But the third story breaks the mold. It breaks the flow. The first two stories are about a single person seeking out an inanimate coin and one oblivious sheep. The third story involves two parties seeking reunion. The third story is about two family members searching for each other. The third story is about two people coming back together.

We read about a son who demanded an early inheritance, skipped town, wasted it all, hit rock bottom, and decided to return home in hopes that he could work as one of his father's hired hands. The story reads: "So [the son] set off and went to his father. But while he was still far off, his father saw him and was filled with compassion; he ran and put his arms around him and kissed him."[6] The father was so excited to see his son that he cut off his son's rehearsed apology, got a robe, ring, and sandals for him to wear, and declared: "Let us eat and celebrate; for this son of mine was dead and is alive again; he was lost and is found!"[7] So they celebrated—in style.

This is a story about reconciliation.

It is about two people reconstructing community.

It is about two people actively seeking to restore their relationship with one another.

This third story is often referred to as the parable of the prodigal son—and for good reason. Prodigal can be defined as "recklessly extravagant,"[8] and the son acted in a very prodigal way. He went off and squandered his inheritance away in a few flashy, pathetic moments. The son was obviously recklessly extravagant.

The son acted in a prodigal way; however, so did the father. The father is recklessly extravagant too, but in a very different way. The father in this story seems to embody the radical nature of God's grace. The prodigal father is recklessly extravagant with the forgiving, merciful grace he extends to his prodigal son when he comes home.

They both act in prodigal ways.

They both are recklessly extravagant.

Grace abounds.

Reconciliation happens.

And this is how it often seems to work. There is a prodigal incident that drives two parties away before there is a recklessly extravagant grace offered and accepted by the people involved. Reconciliation happens.

It is never easy. People can be hurtful. People can be mean. People can be vindictive. But reconciliation is moving past all of that, freeing yourself, forgiving that other person, allowing grace to permeate your relationship, and entering back into community with one another.

And sometimes *we* do the bad stuff. Sometimes *we* are the mean, hurtful, vindictive party. All I will say is that a humble posture and simple apology can go a long way. God is still willing to reconcile with us through Jesus after all we have done, so anything is possible. Forgive yourself and allow others to do the same. Give it a try. Give it a chance.

To seek reconciliation is a holy endeavor. It is needed in every community. It is needed as we continue to be set apart with each other. Without it, we would all just be angry, bitter, bound people. Without it, all relationships would be in ruins. Without it, we would all be alone.

Be holy.

Work on community restoration.

Reconcile.

***

Do you know how to make a politician squirm?

Ask them a difficult question about their faith during a primary.

In 2007, in the heat of the Democratic primary, George Stephanopoulos hosted a political debate on "Principles & Values." And in front of a live crowd and a nationally televised audience, each of the hopeful presidential candidates was asked an incredibly tough fourth question: "My question is to understand each candidate's view of a personal God. Do they believe that, through the power of prayer, disasters like Hurricane Katrina or the Minnesota bridge collapse could have been prevented or lessened?"[9]

Tough question. Not easy to skirt. Not easy to avoid. But it was fascinating to watch each of the politicians try to get around it. There were a lot of allusions to "love" and "mystery" and "God," but not many attempts to answer the question.

What do you think?

What is the power of prayer?

Can prayer prevent tragedies?

A lot of people get confused between the power of prayer and the power of God. Do your prayers change things? Or does God change things? Do you control what happens through your requests and petitions? Or does our listening God control what happens? Some of each? All of the above?

Sara Miles—author, speaker, founder and director of The Food Pantry—has written about the limitations and the power of prayer. She has spent a lot of time with many people in their more tender moments of life: when they were handed a diagnosis, when they received the test results, when they got the bad news. She was often asked to pray in these moments, and over the course of time, she learned more about what she was praying for in each of these situations:

> "Prayer does not cure tuberculosis or Down syndrome. Prayer does not cure mental illness. Prayer can't even cure a common cold. Prayer can't cure. All prayer can do is heal, because healing comes embedded in relationships, and prayer is one of the deepest forms of relationship—with God and with other people. And through relationships, there can be healing in the absence of cure."[10]

I believe in the power of God more than I believe in the power of prayer. But prayer does have power—prayer has real, transforming, healing, uniting power. Prayer connects us to our Creator—it helps us see God's plan and God's perspective on life. Prayer also connects us to each other—it reminds us who and what is important.

Prayer offers us healing and wholeness in the midst of crisis and destruction. It does not have the power to cure us of everything. It does not have the power to prevent all the disasters in life. But it does have real power to transform communities, heal relationships, and link us together in holy ways.

James 5:16b: "[P]ray for one another so that you may be healed."

Ephesians 6:18c: "[A]lways persevere in supplication for all the saints."

So pray for each other. Pray for all the saints. Your words do not have to be well constructed or perfect—they just need to be authentic and genuine. Lift up your worries, anxieties, stresses. Your concerns, requests, and pleas. Your love, joy, and celebrations. Your friends, family, and world. Lift them up to the God who knows you, loves you, and listens to you. Prayer is only useful when it is real. Prayer is only holy when it is true.

Prayer builds community.

Prayer heals relationships.

Be holy.

Pray.

***

Depending on the last time and place you attended worship, you might have celebrated the Lord's Supper, or taken Eucharist, or had Communion. These are all one-in-the-same, just dubbed with different names. And Christians believe that this act—taking the bread and the cup, the body and the blood of Christ—transcends all time and space. It is a simple act with a complicated explanation.

In this act, we are lifted up into the presence of God, surrounded by the great cloud of witnesses, and united with all who do the same. Communion links us with people all over the globe who go to the table. The Eucharist connects us to everyone who has gone before us and will come after us who receive the elements. We celebrate the Lord's Supper where we are, and in the Upper Room with Jesus and the disciples.

We do this to look back and remember God's story. We do this to look forward and anticipate God's ending. We do this to look around and realize we are a part of God's narrative.

There is a tremendous sense of community in this act.

There is a belonging like no other in this act.

And there is a communal call to action in this act.

John Paul II—Pope of the Roman Catholic Church from 1978 to 2005—once prayed these words:

> Lord Jesus, Who in the Eucharist make your dwelling among us and become our traveling companion, sustain our Christian communities so that they may be ever more open to listening and accepting your Word. May they draw from the Eucharist a renewed commitment to spreading in society, by the proclamation of your Gospel, the signs and deeds of an attentive and active charity."[11]

Not only are we reminded of our intimate connection to our Holy God, and not only are we connected to each other in holy ways—we are also reminded of our holy calling to be in and for this world.

Be holy.

Eat the bread. Drink from the cup.

Enjoy the meal that has been set apart.

Enjoy the meal that reminds us that we too are set apart.

***

The prophet Malachi spoke to the people of Judah in the eighth century
B.C. He spoke out against injustice, indecency, and individualism. He
reminded them of their need for God, but also for each other. Malachi
gives a rally cry for community when he poses these questions: "Have we
not all one Father? Did not one God create us? Why do we profane the
covenant of our fathers by breaking faith with one another?"[12]

We crave community.

We need to belong somewhere.

We really do.

So what is stopping us?

Brené Brown—a research professor who has appeared on PBS, NPR,
TED, CNN (and other three-capital-letter corporations)—has done a lot to
study us. She analyzes human beings. She examines the human condition.
And she focuses especially on the areas of courage, authenticity, and
vulnerability. She affirms some of our basic claims: "You are imperfect,
you are wired for struggle, but you are worthy of love and belonging."[13]
Then she goes on to explain how you can discover and keep this sense
of belonging:

> Authenticity is a collection of choices that we have to make every
> day. It's about the choice to show up and be real. The choice to
> be honest. The choice to let our true selves be seen.[14]

Being who you are is a choice you constantly make. Living into your
identity is a choice you repeatedly make. And it is the same with your
connectional nature. Being in community is a choice that you constantly
make. Living into your relationships is a choice you repeatedly make. That
is how you find belonging. You choose to.

We make choices every day that move us closer or further from each other.
We might not always think of our actions in this way, but that is what we
do. We choose to reach out to people. We choose to ignore someone. We
choose to go to social gatherings. We choose to shy away from others.

So why not choose to invest in community?

So why not choose to be more relational?

So why not choose to be more connected?

It can be scary to put ourselves out there. It can be intimidating to
meet others. But it is worth it. We were created in community and for

community. We have a communal calling. We are supposed to spend some time together. It takes courage. It takes vulnerability. It takes authenticity. And we can do it.

Go for it. Dive in. Join a group. Invest time in others. Be proactive and think ahead about ways to spend more time with more people. Be physically and emotionally present when you are with them. Be engaging. Ask questions. Call up an old friend to see how they are doing. Write a handwritten thank you letter to show your appreciation. Volunteer to organize an event. Host a party.

Whatever you do, just make sure you do something. Make the choice to take a step towards community. Be bold and take that step. Some people call this a step of trust. Some people call this a step of faith. Some people call this a step in holiness.

Be holy.

Be bold.

Invest in community.

***

At times we find ourselves living an isolated existence in a lonely world. We have all felt the pain of loneliness. We are a part of a culture that misunderstands it, fails to identify it, and lacks in offering productive ways of expressing it.

We have all felt alone.

But we are never all alone.

We are created in community with one another. We are created to be for each other—to help, to support, to continue building our relationships. We are called as one body. We are invited to be holy partners in our heavenly calling. We are called to be holy.

We are to be set apart with all that is holy. We are to live set apart with each other. We are to intentionally practice what it means to live in Christian community with one another: forgive, reconcile, pray, find church, participate in the sacred meal. Make the choice to invest in your community. It is not always easy to live or be with others, but that is our calling.

Be holy.

Find belonging.

set apart for…

find purpose

chapter 10—aimless

"If you could live forever, what would you live for?"
— *Stephenie Meyer*

"Without God, life has no purpose,
and without purpose, life has no meaning.
Without meaning, life has no significance or hope."
— *Rick Warren*

"Do not run aimlessly."
— *1 Corinthians 9:26*

Charles Lutwidge Dodgson—better known by his pseudonym, Lewis Carroll—was an English writer in the nineteenth century. Dodgson was known for his witty word play and uncanny ability to mix logic with fantasy. Dodgson was more than just an author, though. He was also a brilliant mathematician who could handle complexity. He was a proficient photographer with an eye for capturing and sharing beauty. And he was an ordained deacon.

Dodgson was ordained within the Anglican Church in 1861. He went to school for this and continued his schooling with a goal of becoming a full-fledged priest. And although he completed the program and all his requirements, he never took the vows of the priesthood. He remained a deacon, but did not become a priest. We do not know why Dodgson decided this. We do not know why he chose against becoming a priest. But we do know he lived this faith through his writing.

You probably know Dodgson through his most famous book: *Alice's Adventures in Wonderland*. In this tale, an imaginary girl in an imaginary world helps us discover some real truth about our real lives. Midway through her journey, she stops to ask for some guidance and direction from the Cheshire Cat.

Alice: Would you tell me, please, which way I ought to go from here?
Cat: That depends a good deal on where you want to get to.
Alice: I don't much care where—
Cat: Then it doesn't matter which way you go.[1]

Alice wanders aimlessly throughout this wonderland. How many of us feel like we are wandering aimlessly throughout life? Dodgson's writings bring up some of the most basic and profound questions that we all ask. Where to? What now? Which way?

You see, life is full of twists and turns. It is easy to get confused. It is common to get turned around. And when that happens, we do not always know where we are or which way we ought to go. The path we are following seems to disappear, our vision of the future starts to become fuzzy, and our way forward appears complicated and sometimes impossible. So we stop and ask the questions that we all ask.

Where to?

What now?

Which way?

***

Have you ever been sitting in a room and wondered: "Why am I here?"

I am a pastor. And part of my job as a pastor is to sit in meetings. I attend a lot of long, boring, tedious seminars. I go to a lot of dreary, dull, endless conferences. And in the midst of them, I often find myself asking this question: "Why am I here?"

To be clear, I am not talking about those occasions when I get to sit down with someone and hear his or her story. I am not talking about those instances when I am invited into the more fragile moments of a family. I am not even talking about those times when a group of people gets together with an agenda to accomplish something. I like those meetings. I enjoy those meetings. I feel like a pastor in those meetings.

It is the other meetings I am talking about. Those meetings in which only half the people show up, no one has a plan, a goal is never agreed upon, the coffee is cold, the cookies are stale, and everyone leaves with the sad realization that they will never get those wasted moments of life back. I am talking about those mind-numbing, soul-sucking meetings. I am talking about those meetings in which you sit there and wonder: "Why am I here?"

Patrick Lencioni wrote a leadership fable titled "Death by Meeting." He plainly states that meetings are not inherently bad, but concedes that intense boredom is too often the typical experience of them. If a company or organization holds an hour-long weekly board meeting that accomplishes nothing, that is a tremendous waste. Not only is it an hour wasted, but multiply that hour by how many people are in that room to see how much time was actually wasted. A business owner once told me he stopped his weekly staff meetings because he did the math and saw how much per hour those meetings were costing him in the salaries of the other people sitting around the table. Any meeting that costs several thousands of dollars (or even dozens of volunteered hours) had better be worthwhile. Any meeting in which members cannot identify why they are there, discuss what is really going on, or participate in something significant should be cancelled. Many meetings are meaningless. Many meetings simply cause us to sit in a room and wonder: "Why am I here?"

But the real problem is that this does not just happen in meetings. Sometimes this happens in life.

Søren Kierkegaard—nineteenth-century poet, critic, theologian, and existentialist—did much to help us think about the universal human longing for meaning and purpose. And Kierkegaard bluntly says what we have all secretly thought:

> Where am I? Who am I?
> How did I come to be here?
> What is this thing called the world?
> How did I come into the world?
> Why was I not consulted?
> And If I am compelled to take part in it, where is the director?
> I want to see him.[2]

It is common to think about the larger meaning of life. It is normal to ponder our purpose for being. It is part of our make-up to be curious about these questions. These thoughts are universal. These thoughts make us human. Everyone has said at one point or another: "Why am I here?"

But we do not consistently ask this question.

So we do not always get an answer.

Why am I here?

And if we do not know the starting point of our journey, we will continue to wander aimlessly.

***

Have you ever looked around and thought: "Where am I going?"

I remember playing hide-and-go-seek with my cousins one night at their new house in California. I was only about seven years old. I was the youngest one playing. They were all older and cooler (and braver) than I was. So I thought it was awesome that I got to play with them—until the time came for me to be "it."
I remember throwing a fit and quitting the game. I did not want to be "it." I did not want to have everyone else run away and hide. I did not want them to do this because I was scared. It was a dark, empty, unfamiliar, creepy neighborhood. I did not want to count, turn around, and see nobody. The thought of it terrified me.

But as I tried to quit and go inside, they dragged me back, threw me in the corner, and told me to start counting anyway. So I counted, turned around, and proceeded to completely freak out.

I looked and saw no one. The streets were quiet. The lights were dim. I was spooked. I did not know what to do. I did not know which way to go. So I just started running. I think I figured that I would eventually run past one of them, see them, tag them, and then my turn would be done. But I was so desperate to get it all over with that I just took off without thinking and without any clue where I was going.

My cousins had no idea what I was doing. They saw their opportunity to sneak back to base and so they took it. Once they all made it back, they waited for me to return. But I did not return. So they waited a little longer. And I still did not return.

They kept waiting.

And I kept running.

One of my cousins finally spotted me a couple of blocks away and shouted, "Where are you going?" I was so relieved to hear his voice that I stopped, turned around, ran to him, smiled, and gave him a hug while I said: "You're it." Then I made him walk me back to his house. #strategy

I had no idea where I was going, but I meant to get there quick. I still do this sometimes. I do not normally run away during a game of hide-and-seek, but I still sometimes take off without knowing where I am going. I get antsy and leave. I feel restless and start moving. I get impatient and just take off without thinking about where it is that I am going.

I do this when I feel uncomfortable. I do this when I feel self-conscious. I do this in the moments when I feel unsure and do not know what else to do. I still do this sometimes. Do you?

Thomas Merton—Catholic monk, writer, and mystic—was known for his passion and intensity. He was serious when it came to social justice issues. He was one who had strong ideas about where God was calling us. He was one who helped others discover where God wanted them to go. But even Merton had times in which he was confronted with that feeling of aimless wandering:

> My Lord God, I have no idea where I am going. I do not see the road ahead of me. I cannot know for certain where it will end. Nor do I really know myself, and the fact that I think that I am following your will does not mean that I am actually doing so.[3]

We have all done this. We have all taken off without thinking. We have all started running without discernment. We have all left without knowing where we are going. We have all asked the question at one time or another: "Where am I going?"

But we do not consistently ask this question.

So we do not always get an answer.

Where am I going?

If we do not know the direction of our journey, we will continue to wander aimlessly.

***

Have you ever stopped to ask the question: "Why?"

My youngest daughter does. A lot. She is two years old and "why" is her new favorite word. Our typical conversations go something like this:

"Okay, darling, it's time to pick up your toys."

"Why, Daddy?"

"Because it's time to pick up your toys."

"But why?"

"Just pick up your toys."

"Why?"

"Pick up your toys!"

"Why?!"

"Because I said so!! Now do it!!"

Now I am not saying that my wife is a better parent than I am. (I will let you draw that accurate conclusion on your own.) But I am saying that she handles the question of "why?" better than I typically do. She would respond to the same questions by saying, "Because all the toys need to be in their place… Because we do not want anyone to trip over them… Because we do not want anyone to get hurt and it is nice to have a clean house."

While I just get frustrated and annoyed, my wife actually answers the question. She takes the time to explain it. She injects meaning into the activity. She gives it a purpose. She tells our daughter why. #parenting101

People everywhere need this. It is not just for my two year old.

People need meaning injected into life.

People want to find a purpose for what they do.

People want to know why.

Viktor Frankl understood this in a profound way. He was a well-known Austrian neurologist and psychiatrist who developed something called logotherapy—a type of existential analysis that asserts that our greatest yearning as human beings is to find purpose in our lives. Frankl describes this search as the most powerful and motivating force within each of us.

Frankl was also a Holocaust survivor. On the 25th of September 1942, Frankl was deported with his wife, brother, and parents by the Nazi regime. He was separated from them, transferred around, and moved from camp to camp until he was liberated by the Americans on April 27, 1945. Upon his release, Frankl discovered that he was the only member of his family to survive the concentration camps.

Frankl's philosophy was not some abstract, vague notion he espoused. Frankl discovered his theories from his real world experience. Frankl developed his theories from his real life encounters. He pondered the meaning of life within death camps. Frankl knew it and lived it when he wrote: "[E]verything can be taken from a man but one thing: the last of the human freedoms—to choose one's attitude in any given set of circumstances, to choose one's own way."[4]

And this is why you need a purpose.

We all know that you cannot control all that happens to you. The external circumstances that surround you might be manageable or avoidable in some ways, but not completely. Things will happen to you in life. Things beyond you will affect you. But there is always a space between what happens to you and how you respond it. You might not be in control of everything, but you can choose to control your response. And it is in choosing how you respond that you reveal whether or not you have meaning and purpose in life.

Life is never unbearable unless you have no purpose—then it is often more than you can handle.

You need to know why, or you are going to give up.

You need a purpose, or you will never make it.

***

Wandering through life aimlessly is a good way to get to the end of your life wondering how you got there. If you never stop to think about why you are where you are, then you will never know. If you refuse to look ahead to what is before you, then you will get turned around. Wandering aimlessly is a good way to feel overwhelmed, exhausted, and overloaded. Wandering aimlessly is a good way to make life difficult.

Discovering your purpose is a good way to embrace meaning and commitment within your life. If you often pause to look around, look behind, and look ahead, you will know where you are, where you came from, and where you are going. If adjustments need to be made, you can make them. If a new way forward needs to be found, you can find it. Discovering your purpose is a good way to feel renewed, refreshed, and reinvigorated. Discovering your purpose is a good way to make life worth living.

The purpose of life is simply living a life of purpose.

But discovering your purpose can be complicated.

Today is January 22. (Or at least that is the date I wrote these words.) We are now three weeks and one day into the New Year. At the beginning of every calendar year, people have lofty dreams and high hopes for the next twelve months. Many have sat down and come up with what they think they need to accomplish that year. Some make a list. Others keep it in their heads. Some make it a group effort. Others try to do it all alone. But we all call these our New Year's resolutions.

And every person who makes a serious resolution intends to keep it. They all plan to do it. They all want to follow through with it. But the average New Year's resolution will never make it to the three week mark. The majority of these resolutions are abandoned within twenty-one days. Most people have given up on their resolutions as I write these words—just three weeks after they began.

Researchers say the primary reason for this is lack of clarity. If people are not clear about what they are committing themselves to, then they stand little to no chance of accomplishing it.

Do you know the number one New Year's resolution every year? To lose weight.

This is our case in point. This is where we find our lack of clarity. How much weight do you want to lose? Are you measuring it by percentage lost? Are you measuring it in pounds lost? Are you measuring it in body mass index? Will your eating habits change? Are you going to eat less? Are you going to eat healthier? Or are you going to eat less *and* eat healthier—What does that look like? Are you going to work out? Will you be lifting weights? Will you focus on cardio exercises? How often will you be working out? What time will you set aside to be working out? On what days will you set aside that time to be working out?

If you cannot answer these questions, then you have a problem. You are lacking focus. You are lacking a plan. You are lacking clarity. And if you are lacking these things then you will probably have given up on your New Year's resolution by today—January 22.

We need to continue to ask for clarity as we try to discover of purpose.

My sister and I have always truly enjoyed a good Easter egg hunt. This love of the hunt began when we were young. We would hide and find empty plastic eggs for months after Easter. It was well into the summer before we would even consider allowing our parents to put them away.

As we aged, we got better and worse at the same time. We became better at hiding the eggs. We became very creative and more advanced when it was our turn to hide the eggs. My sister actually was the pioneer when it came to hiding eggs inside the air conditioning vents of the house, but I was the first to start melting and reshaping the eggs. #innovators

But we got worse at finding the eggs. We became so good at hiding the eggs that we consequentially became very bad at finding all of them. It got to the point at which we would have to limit the number of hidden eggs and make notes as to where they were hidden. This way we could go back and double-check if our sibling failed to find them all.

The last year I remember this tradition being in full force, my sister was only allowed to hide ten eggs at a time and I remember being stuck at only 9 eggs for hours. I searched the house, the yard, and the ventilation system to no avail. I was on the hunt for something that I just could not find. I was looking for something that seemed impossible.

I knew it was there.

I believed it existed.

I just could not find it.

How many of us have felt like this about our purpose? We know it is there. We believe it exists. We just cannot find it. We have looked, we have searched, we have hunted for our purpose in this world, but to no avail. It gets frustrating after a while. It gets disheartening after a while. But if we quit looking for our purpose, how will we ever find it?

We need to continue to search so that we can discover our purpose.

Ryan Gosling—Canadian actor, director, and musician—received a lot of media attention a while back from an interview he had with *GQ* magazine. He said:

> The problem with Hollywood is that nobody works. They have meals. They go to Pilates. But it's not enough. So they do drugs. If everybody had a pile of rocks in their backyard and spent every day moving them from one side of the yard to the other, it would be a much happier place.[5]

People need to feel like there is a reason to get up in the morning. People need to experience a sense of accomplishment from time to time. People need to be working towards something or they will stop caring. We are innately created with this need to produce, make, yield, labor—to work.

This innately created need to work is even more pronounced for those of us with a Christian worldview. If we truly see the world as a place where God is active, moving, and continually recreating, then there is plenty of work for us to participate in and enjoy. God does not have us work because God needs us to work; rather, God invites us to work because we need to work. And it is through this kingdom work that we can fine tune and better reveal our purpose.

We need to continue to do the work of God so that we can discover our purpose.

Discovering your purpose can be complicated—but it is worth it.

***

The longest recorded sermon of Jesus in the Bible is found in the book of Matthew. Chapters 5 through 7 are referred to as the "Sermon on the Mount." The text tells us that Jesus walks up the side of a mountain, sits down with his disciples, and starts teaching. It is a fairly comprehensive teaching. It covers the gamut of the Christian life. It shows the full spectrum of our calling.

Towards the end of this teaching, Jesus tells us to do three things: ask, seek, and knock. We read:

> "Ask and it will be given to you; seek and you will find; knock and the door will be opened to you. For everyone who asks receives; the one who seeks finds; and to the one who knocks, the door will be opened."[6]

Ask. Seek. Knock. Easy enough to remember. Difficult enough to shy away from.

Scholars talk about the boldness of these three verbs. To ask for what you want expecting to receive something. To actively seek what you are looking for while you anticipate a discovery. To knock on a door and assume that it will be opened for you.

If you do these things, you are either setting yourself up for a big failure or a tremendous success. And the result of your asking all depends on who you are asking, with whom you are seeking, and the one who happens to be on the other side of that door.

The world has disappointed me a lot. I no longer expect to get what I ask for in this world. I do not anticipate finding what I am seeking from it. Nor do I assume doors will magically be opened for me if I knock long enough and loud enough. But God surprises me constantly—especially when I ask, seek, and knock in relation to my purpose. If we ask for clarity when it comes to our purpose, should we not expect that we will get it? If we are actively seeking our purpose, should we not anticipate that we will find it? If we are out constantly knocking on doors and working with God, should we not assume that we will see it?

When it comes to discovering our purpose, maybe we need to be bold and just keep going.

Ask with expectation.

Seek with anticipation.

Knock with assumption.

Discover your purpose.

***

We are called to be holy.

We are invited to live our life set apart from, with, and for. We find our identity in being set apart from all that is unholy. We find our belonging in being set apart with all who are holy. And we find our purpose in being set apart for God in this world.

And it is this last aspect of holiness—to be set apart for—that is perhaps the most important. Because that is where we find meaning for our lives. That is where we discover our purpose. That is our "why." It is in being set-apart-for that we find guidance and direction as we continue the journey.

Consider the way Paul embraces this sense of being set-apart-for. Paul wrote in Romans 1 that he was "a servant of Jesus Christ, called to be an apostle, set apart for the gospel of God."[7] Set apart for the gospel of God—the good news. Set apart for apostleship—one who is sent out. Set apart for a purpose—a life with meaning worth living.

You too are set apart for a reason.

You too are set apart intentionally.

Be holy.

Find purpose.

chapter 11—balance

"Oh Lord, I'm still not sure what I stand for.
What do I stand for?"
—FUN

"The Lord will fulfill his purpose for me;
your steadfast love, O Lord, endures forever."
—Psalm 138:8

"It's not enough to have lived.
We should be determined to live for something."
—Winston Churchill

As soon as I finished my seminary degree, I had to complete my ordination requirements. One of those requirements was that I take a unit of CPE.

CPE stands for Clinical Pastoral Education. It's basically boot camp for pre-pastors. It is a program in which they put you in very intense situations. They require you to be present in the awkward moments of life. And then they ask you to remind people of God's presence in the midst of it all.

I did my unit of CPE in Atlanta, and found myself serving in several inner-city ministry outreach programs. During the first week of the program we were invited to see all the locations, tour all of the facilities, and meet the people who worked there. Some of the sites were impressive. Some of the ministries were remarkable. But most all of it was very depressing at first glance.

These were tough placements with people in tough phases of life. The homeless and the displaced. The prostitutes and the gang members. The drugs and addictions. The violence and injustice.

I still remember meeting the director of Atlanta's largest homeless outreach and advocacy center. He introduced himself to us. He thanked us for coming. And he told us about the mission of that place. He told us about the importance of his faith. He told us about the importance of this ministry. He told us about the importance of the volunteers who came. He said he would always go to welcome the volunteers personally and ask them two questions: "Where are you from? And why are you here?"

Most of the time they would respond by stating the name of their church or hometown. And then almost everyone would respond with what they were there to do that day: help in the kitchen, file paperwork, answer phones, check the doors, etc.

Notice what happened.

He asked "why" they were there.

They responded with "what" they would be doing.

He called these responders "short-term volunteers" and he said if volunteers are not crystal clear as to why they were there, then they would be gone within the week. "This ministry is tough. This work is dirty. And if you are not of the understanding that God is calling you into this mess, you will be out of here quick."

At this point, all of us CPE students were speechless, frozen, and very intimidated.

So he continued to talk and told us a story—a story about a volunteer who responded in a different way. The director asked the typical two questions, waited for the typical two responses—but was surprised by what he heard.

When he asked: "Why are you here?" she responded: "Because God's here. And there's a lot of love here."

The director pointed to the lady busily moving in the background and then said: "And she's been here with us for over twenty years."

Sometimes that is all it takes.

Recognize God in our midst.

Feel the abundance of love.

And you find a purpose worth sustaining.

Whatever your purpose might be and however it takes shape in your life, it will always fit the universal pattern of love: love God, love neighbor, and love ourselves.

***

Towards the end of the gospel of Matthew, Jesus is confronted once again by some of the religious leaders of his day. After some of the Sadducees fail to silence him, the Pharisees get together to give it a try. They ask: "Teacher, which is the greatest commandment in the Law?"[1]

Right away we know this is a trap.

The Pharisees and the Sadducees were both experts in using the Law— the Torah—the first five books of the Bible. They were not asking this question because they themselves were curious; they were asking this question in hopes that they could discredit and embarrass Jesus. They were trying to trap Jesus and force him to give a simple answer to a complex question.

But Jesus is smooth. No one ever traps Jesus. He does not simply answer their one basic question, but responds to their challenge on multiple levels. He finds yet another way to silence them. Jesus replies:

> "Love the Lord your God with all your heart and with all your soul and with all your mind." This is the first and greatest commandment. And the second is like it: "Love your neighbor as yourself." All the Law and the Prophets hang on these two commandments."[2]

Jesus is quoting the Law here. This is what they expected. This is what they wanted. They wanted Jesus to stake a claim by proclaiming what he thought was the most important, most crucial, most vital aspect of the Law. And he does. Jesus tells them (and us) that the primary commandment is to "love the Lord your God."[3] But Jesus keeps going. Jesus does not stop. Jesus continues to explain the Law to them. He goes on to complete the summary of what the Law is all about—"love your neighbor as yourself."[4]

You see, for these Pharisees and Sadducees, the Law was used to trap people. The Law was used to condemn people. The Law was used to serve their own interests and take care of their unwanted problems. They were experts in using the Law, but they were ignorant in knowing what the Law was really all about.

The Law was first given back in the day when the Israelites were trying to figure out what it meant to be in community with one another. They were newly escaped slaves from Egypt, on a journey to the land God was giving them, and they were wandering aimlessly throughout the wilderness.

The Law gave them hope.

The Law gave them meaning.

The Law gave them a purpose.

The Law gave them a way to live together, to serve together, to love together. The Law was not a trap used to condemn each other; it was a guidepost to show them all the way forward. And the Law was only ever given to God's people after God created them, promised to be with them, delivered them, took care of them, and loved them. The Law came after all of this, so the Law should never be used to judge or trap each other; it should only ever be used to reveal God's purpose and love for us all.

And so Jesus summarized the Law for us in his response. The first two points are easy to see: love God and love neighbor. The words "as yourself"[5] give us the third. It is very subtle. It is often missed. But we are also called to love ourselves.

So in this summary, Jesus is giving us what the Law has always given God's people.

Jesus is giving us hope.

Jesus is giving us meaning.

Jesus is giving us a purpose.

Love God. Love neighbor. Love yourself.

***

Jesus begins by quoting from *the Shema* in his response. The word *shema* is Hebrew for "hear" and that is where the original scripture quote begins in Deuteronomy 6:

> Hear, O Israel: The Lord our God, the Lord is one. Love the Lord your God with all your heart and with all your soul and with all your strength.[6]

Jesus begins his summary of the Law with reference to the Shema. This passage was and still is an important part of the Jewish faith and tradition. It is used in both morning and evening prayer services. It is one of the earliest memorized scripture passages for their children. And the reason for this is because of what comes next. The Shema continues:

> These commandments that I give you today are to be on your hearts. Impress them on your children. Talk about them when you sit at home and when you walk along the road, when you lie down and when you get up. Tie them as symbols on your hands

and bind them on your foreheads. Write them on the doorframes
of your houses and on your gates.[7]

The Shema reminds us of what is most important. It reminds us to love
God. It helps us to never forget. You can still find people of the Jewish
tradition with this passage written on their doorframes and inscribed
above their beds and stuck in the little crevasses of their fences. And the
traditional *Shema* prayer concludes with another passage, from Numbers
15: "So you shall remember and do all my commandments, and you shall
be holy to your God."[8]

So love God. Be holy. Do not forget.

Back in the 1640s, post-Reformation, a large group of Christians got
together to try to clarify what they in particular believed about loving their
God and living their faith. They were called the Westminster Assembly.
They were a sanctioned group that was recognized by several governments
and many denominations.

They spent over five years together. They put out only three documents.
Needless to say, they put a lot of effort and energy into every word they
produced. And one of the documents that came out of this assembly is
called the Westminster Shorter Catechism. These are the first two lines
from it:

Q. What is the chief end of man?
A. Man's chief end is to glorify God, and to enjoy him forever.[9]

Before they asked any other question, before they introduced any other
topic, and without even so much as a general introduction, the Westminster
Assembly asserted what they thought was the purpose of humanity—our
chief end, our main goal, our primary reason for being: to glorify and
enjoy God forever.

We definitely are to glorify God. Consider Romans 11: "For from him
and through him and to him are all things. To him be the glory forever.
Amen."[10] A similar directive is found in Revelation 4:11: "You are worthy,
our Lord and God, to receive glory and honor and power, for you created
all things."[11] And in 1 Corinthians 10 Paul writes: "whatever you do, do
everything for the glory of God."[12]

We definitely should enjoy God forever. Here are a few examples: Psalm
144: "Happy are the people whose God is the Lord.[13] Luke 2: "Do not
be afraid; for see—I am bringing you good news of great joy for all the
people."[14] Philippians 4: "Rejoice in the Lord always; again I will say,
Rejoice."[15]

This is what we read throughout our story. This is what we see throughout our lives. Rick Warren—a pastor, author, and motivator—rephrases it all in this way: "The smile of God is the goal of your life."[16]

Glorify and enjoy God forever.

Make God smile.

Love God.

***

Loving God is pretty straightforward. It seems to be pretty self-explanatory.

But what about loving each other? What about loving yourself? Is loving a person different than loving God? What does loving a person look like? How do you practice healthy self-love? How do you show love to your neighbor? Who is my neighbor?

In Luke, a lawyer asks Jesus this very question: "Who is my neighbor?"[17]

And Jesus gives an enlightening response.

Jesus tells the story of a man traveling from Jerusalem to Jericho who encounters some unfriendly people—and one helpful neighbor. First, he meets some folks who rob him, strip him, beat him, and then leave him to die. Second, a priest walks by, see him lying in agony, and actually walks on the opposite side of the road so he does not have to be too close to this dying man. Third, a Levite also walks by him, sees him writhing with pain, and also crosses to the opposite side of the road to stay away from him.

But, finally, a Samaritan walks by the man, sees him lying there, and is moved with pity. The Samaritan postpones his travels, cleans and bandages this man's wounds, and takes him to a nearby inn. The Samaritan then pays the innkeeper to take care of this man and to watch over him in his fragile state.

Jesus then stops the story and asks, "Which of these three, do you think, was a neighbor to the man who fell into the hands of the robbers?"[18] The lawyer knew the obvious answer and so do we. The Samaritan was the neighbor. The Samaritan was the one who showed him mercy, care, compassion. The Samaritan was the one who showed him love.

Now a couple of noteworthy things take place in this story. We find a surprising protagonist. The hero of the story is not who we expected it to be. The priest is not the one who shows kindness. The Levite—who comes from a long religious lineage—is not the one who shows empathy. It is the Samaritan who ends up saving the day. The Samaritan—the one who lives in a foreign land, the one who is despised by the Israelites, the one they view as less than human–is the neighbor, who we are supposed to be like.

The Samaritan was an unexpected neighbor.

Who are our unexpected neighbors?

The other surprising aspect of this story is that we find something we could easily do. The Samaritan does not use superpowers to heal this man. He does not have to fight back the robbers, the wild animals, or the elements of nature. He does something that we could actually replicate. He sets an example that we could follow.

Too many Christians in this world are trying to be Jesus. We are called to be holy and to be set apart for Jesus, but we are not called to be another Jesus. We already have a Jesus. We do not need a second. He is more than enough.

And, besides, the role of Jesus is a role that we could never live up to. Jesus is the one who says: "I am the good shepherd. The good shepherd lays down his life for the sheep."[19] And Jesus is the one who says: "I am the bread of life. Whoever comes to me will never go hungry, and whoever believes in me will never be thirsty."[20] Jesus is the light that illuminates the world, the gate through which we are invited, the vine who supplies us with nourishment, the resurrection and the life worth living.[21]

So the Samaritan in this story gives us a model for how we are to love our neighbor. He finds a man lying on the side of the road, takes the time to bandage and clean him up, takes the man to a place where he can receive some help, and then makes sure that he receives the help he needs. This is what we are asked to do.

We are not expected to be Jesus. We are not able to be Jesus. We cannot do everything for everybody. When we try to do this, we are no help for anybody. When we try to do this, we fail miserably. When we try to do this, we do not show love to ourselves or them. Stretching yourself too thin with the false hopes of being a second Jesus is not loving your neighbor, and it is not loving yourself.

Philippians 2 reads: "Each of you should look not only to your own interests, but also to the interests of others."[22] This emphasizes that we are to look after each other, but we are also supposed to look after ourselves. We should not be selfish. We should not be self-centered. But we should take care of ourselves as we take care of others. We should continue to keep our own interests in mind as we keep their interests in mind too.

The Samaritan also did this well. He picked up, bandaged, and delivered the man to a place where he would be taken care of. The Samaritan helped get him to where he needed to be. The Samaritan helped make provisions for him there. But then the Samaritan left.

The Samaritan told the innkeeper: "Take care of him; and when I come back, I will repay you whatever more you spend."[23] The Samaritan had stuff to do. The Samaritan had other things going on. And with his efficient, effective loving way, the Samaritan probably found more people to help later that same day.

The point is that this Samaritan did not let his life fall apart while helping this other man get his life back together. We too should not let our own lives fall apart while helping others. That is not how you take care of your own life. That is not how you look after your own interests. That is not how you show love to yourself. And if you let your own life fall apart, how much help will you really be next time you find someone in need?

The Samaritan should be our model.

Love neighbor. Love yourself.

At the end of this conversation with the lawyer, Jesus says: "Go and do likewise."[24]

So go and do likewise.

***

Go.

Do.

Likewise.

One of the many things I love about Jesus is that he is very action-oriented. Jesus is always on the move. Jesus is always planning something new. Jesus is always busy. And Jesus always invites us to "go and do likewise."[25] Following Jesus is not easy or simple—it is way more fun than that. It is a thrilling adventure. It is a dynamic, quick-paced, ever-changing movement. It is many things—but it is never passive or boring.

Not all religions emphasize this to the same degree. Not all religions are the same. They can have comparable stories. They can have similar emphases. They can even have some related ethical teachings. But they all have slightly different nuances.

The "golden rule" is found in almost every religion in some form or another. It is regarded as one of the most widely known and accepted laws that govern humanity. For those of us who are self-declared, action-oriented Jesus followers—we look to this verse:

> Christianity—"In everything, do to others as you would have them do to you."[26]

But the "golden rule" is not one universal sentence. It is more of a similar strand of thought that continues to reshape and reappear in various places. Almost all the different major religions contain slightly different teachings that revolve around this concept. The following are all taken from the religious writings or teachings of the different religions:

> Buddhism—"Hurt not others in ways that you yourself would find hurtful."[27]

> Hinduism—"This is the sum of duty: Do naught unto others which would cause you pain if done to you."[28]

> Judaism—"What is hateful to you, do not to your fellow man."[29]

> Confucianism—"Surely it is the maxim of loving-kindness: Do not unto others what you would not have them do unto you."[30]

> Zoroastrianism—"That nature alone is good which refrains from doing unto another whatsoever is not good for itself."[31]

> Islam—"No one of you is a believer until he desires for his brother that which he desires for himself."[32]

> Taoism—"Regard your neighbor's gain as your own gain and your neighbor's loss as your own loss."[33]

What similarities do you find in these? What differences do you notice? What difference does it make? I am not going to get into a long discussion with you about the teachings of other world religions, but I am going to point out something unique to Jesus in this golden list of rules.

Jesus is the only one with a call for action. Jesus is the only one that invites us to go and "do" something. Most of the other religions are asking you to "not do" something—do not cause pain, do not hurt others, do not do what is hateful, do not do what is not good, do not do what you do not want them to do to you. And the ones that are not phrased negatively are phrased passively—regard their gain or loss as your own, desire for them what you desire for yourself.

So contained within the "golden rule" and these ethical teachings of the other major world religions, you are either told to "not do" something or just passively regard and desire. Jesus is the only one who calls us to actively go and do something for our neighbor. Jesus is the only one who invites them to actively go and do something for us. Our calling from Jesus is always an action-oriented invitation.

Love neighbor. Love yourself.

Go. Do.

***

When is the last time you were on a seesaw?

Do you even know what I am talking about? (Some people call a seesaw a teeter-totter—but I always thought that sounded strange.) It is a piece of playground equipment that is long and narrow and has some sort of a pivot point in the middle, so that as one end goes up, the other end goes down.

I have always loved seesaws. I remember learning to play on one when I was a kid. I remember continuing to play on them while I was growing up. And I still play on them today when I get a chance. The playground that my family and I frequent has three seesaws. #thelushlife

But I think seesaws have changed. For some unknown reason, my end always rests on the ground. I put one of my daughters on the other end, and my end remains on the ground. I put both of my daughters at the other end, and my end is still all the way down. I put my wife plus my two daughters on the other end, and I still am sitting in the dirt. This never used to happen to me as a kid, but it always seems to happen to me now. There seems to be some sort of weight imbalance issue we have (I have). #weird

The trickiest part of the seesaw is finding the balance. Playing on one is a lot more fun if a balance can be found between the sides. You can either scoot up to sit in front of the handlebars to lighten your side or you can pile the people together on the other end to make it heavier. But finding that balance can be difficult.

That is the same with our purpose.

Finding the balance is difficult when it comes to our purpose.

We are called to love God, love neighbor, and love ourselves. We are called to do all three of these. Not just one of them. Not just two-and-a-half of them. We are called to do all three. But all too often we do these at the expense of each other. Maybe we love ourselves a little too much and love our neighbor a little too little. Maybe we try to focus all our love on God and ignore the problems of the people around us. Maybe we become too busy loving our neighbor and forget about God. Seminaries teach us about "clergy burnout"—when pastors exert all their energy trying to love God and love neighbor and they in turn neglect their own needs or the needs of their families.

Love God, love neighbor, and love ourselves. It is not an either-or. It is not a multiple-choice. It is an all-of-the-above.

This is why balance is so important. None of these three are mutually exclusive. Many times they overlap and intersect with each other. Many times you can accomplish all three at the same time. But this is not automatic. This is not a given.

Throughout your life you will continually find new ways to live out each of these. You will discover fresh ways to love God, emerging patterns to love neighbor, and new methods to love yourself. Continue to explore and discern your purpose, but be mindful and aware of your balance as you do.

So you have to find the balance—like on a seesaw.

And you have to keep the balance—like on a bicycle.

Do you know how to stay balanced on a bicycle? You keep moving. This too is the same with your purpose. Keep going. Keep moving. Follow the guidance of Holy Spirit. And strive for balance. Let your prayer be like that of Job: let me discover "a just balance, and let God know my integrity!"[34]

***

Proverbs 19 states: "Desire without knowledge is not good, and one who moves too hurriedly misses the way."[35] We cannot go through life wandering aimlessly and expect to wind up where we want to be. We need to stop and take a look at the important questions. Where am I going? Why am I here? What is the meaning of all this?

In the first chapter of James we read: "Do not merely listen to the word, and so deceive yourselves. Do what it says."[36] We must do more than just think about it. We need to ask for clarity, actively seek our calling, and get out there to knock on doors and do the work of the kingdom.

Love God. Love God and never forget who God is and what God has done for us. Glorify and enjoy God forever. Make God smile.

Love neighbor. Love your unexpected neighbors. Love your inconvenient neighbors. Love them, care for them, provide for them—just as you would for yourself.

Love yourself. Do not overstretch yourself. Do not try to be a second Jesus. Do not try to be anything else other than the amazing you that God made you to be.

Go and do. Keep moving. Maintain the balance.

Be holy.

Discover your purpose.

chapter 12—embrace

"We may run, walk, stumble, drive, or fly,
but let us never lose sight of the reason for the journey,
or miss a chance to see a rainbow on the way."
— *Gloria Gaither*

"We know that all things work together for good
for those who love God,
who are called according to his purpose."
— *Romans 8:28*

"Make your work to be in keeping with your purpose."
— *Leonardo da Vinci*

To be holy is to be set apart from, with, and for.

We are to be set apart from. This is where we find our identity. This is what makes us who we are. This is what makes us us, not them. This makes us unique, distinctive, special, different. The more we discern our identity as one known, revealed, and loved by God—the more we realize that we are set apart from—the more we discover who we are.

We are to be set apart with. This is where we find our belonging. This is our communal calling. This is how we know that we are not alone and that we do have others with us on this journey. The more we embrace that we were created in and for community—the more we recognize that we are set apart with—the more we discover our belonging.

We are to be set apart for. This is where we find our purpose. This is our why. This is the meaning and significance in life. This is our reason for being. This is where we must find and keep our balance. The more we love God, love neighbor, and love ourselves—the more we figure out what we are set apart for—the more we discover our purpose.

And it is this last nuance that we must embrace. We have intentionally been set apart for. There is something out there for you to do. There is something out there for you to participate in. There is some purpose out there waiting for you to claim it.

So be holy.

Be set apart for.

Find purpose.

***

A man named Simon Sinek wrote the book *Start with Why*. Your "why" is your purpose. Your "why" is your motivation. Sinek's main premise is that people do not primarily respond to "what" you do or "how" you do, but "why" you do it. People want to know "why." So Sinek argues that we need to learn to start with the "why."

So start with the "why."

All the really effective companies do this—like TOMS Shoes.[1]

Most shoe companies tell you that they sell great shoes (the what) and then they tell you that their shoes will make you run faster and longer (the how). But they neglect to tell you why they do what they do. Are you ready to buy their shoes after reading that? Are you now racing to the shoe store as you read this line? No. Of course not. This will not inspire you to buy shoes. This does not motivate you to participate in what they are doing. This only operates on the first two levels of the what-how-why spectrum.

But TOMS Shoes goes about it all in a very different way. TOMS tells you why they do what they do—and they start there. They begin by telling you that they are on a mission to change the world (the why), they will do this by identifying and fulfilling the needs of children worldwide (the how), and finally they reveal that they just happen to do this by selling shoes to you and donating shoes to children in need (the what). This is more inspiring. This is something more people would like to be involved with.

So the question becomes: "Do you want to change the world with us?"

Rather than: "Do you want to buy some shoes from us?"

This is not to say that other shoe companies do not donate shoes to children or do the same service work that TOMS does, but they do it differently. Others do not invite you to participate in changing the world with them. Others do not invite you to do anything other than spend your money. Others do not start with the why.

All the really effective individuals do this—like Martin Luther King Jr.

There were a lot of people in the Civil Rights Movement who would tell you what you needed to do and how you needed to do it, but few who told you why. This is the reason King was so influential. This is the reason King was able to lead the nation. He led from the why. He gave everything a purpose, a direction, a goal. He helped envision a new future and a better world while inviting others to participate in it. He did not give the "I Have a Step-By-Step Plan" speech, but the "I Have a Dream" speech. He told us why. He started with the why. And he inspired us and invited us to join him.

All the really effective writers do this—like the author of Ephesians.

The church in Ephesus was searching for meaning. They were searching for purpose. They were searching for the why. Why be a Christian? Why tell people about this Jesus fellow? Why should I live my life this way? Why should I try to be holy? The response is found in chapter 4 of the letter to the Ephesians.

The author spends some time with *what* we need to do: "put away your former way of life, your old self" and "clothe yourselves with the new self."[2]

The author also elaborates on *how* we can do it. We see how we can live into our new life: speak the truth, labor and work honestly, contribute to society, share with the needy, control anger, put away all bitterness, be kind, be forgiving.[3]

But the letter does not stop there. It keeps going. We not only hear what the Christian life is and how we can embody it, but most importantly it reminds us *why* we would want to do this. It gives us the meaning. It gives us a purpose. We get the what and the how of it all, but more important is the why.

Notice it does not follow my parenting strategy and say, "because I said so."

It does not even one-up my parenting strategy and say, "because God says so."

It says: "to be like God in true righteousness and holiness."[4]

The author of Ephesians is telling us why. We learn that God is in the business of making us holy. God is one who draws close to us and sets us apart from, with, and for a purpose. Then we get a list of how this happens in our daily life and in our encounters with each other. And finally we get to what the author is talking about—clothing ourselves with the new life. The author is inviting us into a new way of life.

You are called to be holy (the why) through your relationships and interactions (the how) and enter into your new way of life (the what).

All the really effective saints do this—like you.

Know why you do what you do and start from there.

Be holy.

Start with the why.

***

Christians are like manure.

(Keep reading.)

If you spread them out, they can do a lot of good.

But if they just sit around in a pile, they start to stink after a while.

We are not called to sit around. We are not good at sitting around. The original Christians were referred to as "the Way" because they actively followed the way of Jesus. They were not "the Waiters" or "the Stuck." They were a movement. They were going forward. They were known as "the Way" because they would always "go and do." [5]

Sometimes we forget this. Sometimes we ignore this. Sometimes we form a holy huddle. There is nothing wrong with enjoying each other's company. There is nothing wrong with gathering together for study, prayer, or fellowship. But when Christians sit in a holy huddle for too long, we start to argue over silly things, such as flower arrangements and liturgical colors. #adventblue

That is not what we were made for. That is not our purpose. We are called to be set apart for God. We are called to be set apart for God's purposes. We are invited to participate in what God is actively doing in this world right now.

Missio Dei is Latin for the "mission of God." It starts from the premise that God is already at work in our world—renewing, restoring, and reconciling. God is already busy creating and recreating. God is at work fulfilling this mission—and we are invited to join in. So our purpose is to discern God's presence in our midst, figure out how the Spirit is moving among us, and participate in that holy work.

Nothing about that tells us to sit around in a pile.

We should really start to think of ourselves as the "holy diffused" rather than the "holy huddle."

And if we need help finding our purpose, or if we need help finding God's presence, scripture gives us plenty of guidance. The prophet Micah writes to the people of Judah about what their God is doing in their midst and calls them to do it with their God: "What does the Lord require of you but to do justice, and to love kindness, and to walk humbly with your God."[6]

Notice the prepositional phrase at the end of that sentence—"with your God." We are called to do justice, love kindness, and walk humbly. And we are specifically called to do these things with our God. That means God is already busy doing them. We just have to join in.

Jesus tells us his purpose in Luke 4. Jesus went to his hometown of Nazareth, stood up in the synagogue, and quoted the prophet Isaiah: "The Spirit of the Lord is upon me, because he has anointed me to bring good news to the poor. He has sent me to proclaim release to the captives and recovery of sight to the blind, to let the oppressed go free, to proclaim the year of the Lord's favor."[7] We too are all called to this. We too can read these words of Isaiah. We too can do all these things—with Jesus.

And at the end of Matthew, Jesus gives his disciples a commissioning: "Go therefore and make disciples of all nations, baptizing them in the name of the Father and of the Son and of the Holy Spirit, and teaching them to obey everything that I have commanded you."[8]

Jesus gives his disciples their purpose. He does this for his disciples who were present at that moment. He does this for his disciples who are present at this present moment. He does this for his disciples at any given moment. Jesus tells us to go, make other disciples, baptize them, and teach them. But then he says, "And remember, I am with you always, to the end of the age."[9]

God is all around us. God is all throughout this world. We do not have to look very far to see God. And God is at work in this world. The *missio Dei* is alive and well. All we are asked to do is participate, contribute, join in. Because that is where God is—that is how we can be with God.

Be holy.

Participate.

Be with God.

***

Marcus Buckingham—a leadership speaker and business consultant—
has given us a new way to understand our strengths and weaknesses. He
once said: "Your strengths aren't what you're good at and your weaknesses
aren't what your bad at."[10] Your strengths are more than just your interests
or your abilities. And your weaknesses might be areas in which you are
capable or talented.

Buckingham claims that your strengths are what strengthen you. Your
strengths are what make you feel strong. Your strengths are what renew
your energy. Your strengths are what recharge your purpose. Your
strengths are where your hunger is met and your appetite is satisfied.

Your weaknesses are the opposite; they are the things that make you feel
weak. They are what drain you, exhaust you, and overwhelm you. They
are what leave you wanting something more, something better, something
else. You might be good at your weaknesses, but your weaknesses are not
good for you.

Part of the invitation to be holy is figuring out what you have been set
apart for. You were created with an intention. You were made for a reason.
You have been set apart for a purpose.

And your purpose should be a strength.

Your purpose should strengthen you.

Your purpose should leave you refreshed and invigorated.

Katie Davis was a homecoming queen who drove her yellow convertible
all over Brentwood, Tennessee. After she graduated from high school in
2007, she planned on attending college to study nursing. But before she
enrolled, Davis wanted to travel. She wanted to see the world. She wanted
to get some real life experience.

So Katie traveled. But she did not go where anyone expected her to go—
she instead went to Uganda.

Katie signed up to teach kindergarten at an orphanage in a small village
near the town of Jinja. After she had been there a few months, a mud
hut home not far from the orphanage collapsed during a heavy rain. It
caved in on three young girls—AIDS orphans that Katie had met earlier.

One of those children was named Agnes. Agnes was 9 and was taken to
receive medical assistance and Agnes still remembers Katie remaining by
her side the entire time. Katie was with her that night. Katie was with her
while she received medical help. Katie was with her the next few days.

And as an orphaned child who typically had no one to care for her, we can only imagine the impact Katie had on Agnes' life in those moments. #goosebumps

In the midst of all this, Agnes gathered up the courage to ask if she can live with Katie. Having received little from adults her entire life, Agnes' hopes were not high—but she asked anyway. And Katie said yes. #doublegoosebumps

Katie ended up adopting all three of the girls from the incident that night. She moved into a larger house that could accommodate them. She took care of them. She provided for them. She nurtured them. She loved them. None of this was in Katie Davis' plan for her life. This was not her original reason for going to Uganda. This took her by surprise. But that was not the only surprise.

The other surprise was how it made Katie feel. She felt a new kind of energy. She discovered a more determined drive. She found what strengthened her.

Over the next eighteen months, Katie actually adopted ten more girls who were abandoned, abused, or orphaned. Just a couple of years before this, Katie was worried about pep rallies and finals. Now she worries about getting all thirteen of her girls to sit down at the breakfast table together. Katie also serves as the director of a local nonprofit agency she founded, Amazima Ministries, and recently published her first book.

Katie calls herself a Christian and she idolizes Mother Teresa, but she never thought this would be her life. In reflection, she said, "I think that's definitely something that I was made for. God just designed me that way because he already knew that this is what his plan was for my life—even though I didn't."[11]

Davis found her strength. Davis found what strengthened her.

What gives you that new kind of energy? What gives you that more determined drive? What would ignite your passion? What would jumpstart your purpose? Following the invitation to be holy should not be exhausting. It should not be a chore. It should be something that strengthens you. It should be something that makes you feel more alive.

Be holy.

Find your strengths.

***

If you actually dedicate your life to discovering your purpose,...if you actually totally commit yourself to your calling,...if you actually go all in with this invitation—people are going to look at you like you are crazy.

They will stare.

They will whisper.

They might laugh.

But this is more a reflection of the state of our world than it is a reflection of you.

Donald Miller has a way with words. In *A Million Miles in a Thousand Years*, Miller wrote about the story our world often tells us:

> We live in a world where bad stories are told, stories that teach us life doesn't mean anything and that humanity has no great purpose. It's a good calling, then, to speak a better story. How brightly a better story shines. How easily the world looks to it in wonder. How grateful we are to hear these stories, and how happy it makes us to repeat them[12]

Actually claiming and embracing your purpose in life is weird.

People are not used to it. People are not familiar with it. They are not accustomed to that kind of boldness. They are not prepared to react to that kind of confidence. It is uncommon. It is unordinary. It is abnormal. But who wants to be normal anyway? Normal is broke. Normal is broken.

Hélder Câmara, a Roman Catholic Archbishop, writes: "When I give food to the poor, they call me a saint. When I ask why they are poor, they call me a communist."[13] People do not always like it when you challenge the status quo. People do not always like it when you question the world. People do not always like it when you ask why. But who asked them anyway? You are not called to preserve the present state, but to proclaim the good news.

Actually claiming and embracing your purpose in life is holy.

This is because life does have meaning. This is because humanity does have a greater purpose. God calls us to claim it. God calls us to embrace it. God calls us to be set apart for it.

I am done wandering aimlessly. I am done ignoring the questions. I will ask with expectation. I will seek with anticipation. I will knock with assumption. I will go and do. I will love God, love neighbor, love self. I will find the balance. I will keep moving. I will continually discover, refine, and explore my purpose.

Be holy.

Find purpose.

Let them stare.

***

Ham or eggs?

Both are delicious breakfast foods. Both are favorites of mine. Both are typically eaten in my household if I am in charge of the first meal of our day. But I am not asking if you want ham or eggs. I am not asking which one you prefer.

I am asking which you would like to be.

Are you going to be ham or eggs? You see, a pig and a chicken are both used for these breakfast foods—but their participation level is very different.

The chicken contributes a couple of eggs to your breakfast. The chicken had to put in a little effort. The chicken had to work for a bit. But the chicken is just kind of involved in your breakfast. Your breakfast is not of that much concern to her. Your breakfast does not really affect her life all that much.

The pig contributes the ham to your breakfast. The pig is fully committed. The pig gives herself for your breakfast. The pig gives her whole self for your breakfast. This is maximum effort. This is the most the pig could give. Your breakfast is very important to the pig, because your breakfast completely and entirely affects her life.

So ham or eggs?

Fully committed or just involved?

Be ham.

Be holy.

When it comes to your purpose, what is your participation level?

Are you pursuing your purpose with passion? Are you out there actively seeking the *missio Dei*? Are you dedicating your life in the way God intended? Or are you waiting for it to come to you? Are you waiting for your purpose to fall in your lap? Are you being passive? Are you being negative?

What about when it comes to your calling?

What is your participation level in the invitation to be holy?

Be holy.

Two words.

Two words that reveal a better way.

Two words that make a world of difference.

Too many people go through life without actually living it. They constantly live with a yearning for something else, something bigger, something better. But they are not sure how to go about it. They welcome rather than challenge the status quo. They wander aimlessly through life and finally arrive at the feelings of inadequacy, isolation, and insignificance. They strive to be normal. They strive to be ordinary.

But God wants us. God desires us. God longs for us. God chooses to work with us, in us, through us, and among us. God calls us to holiness.

Our Holy God has some holy plans for this world. Our Holy God is action-oriented. Our Holy God is on the move. Our Holy God is actively renewing, restoring, and reconciling all things. And our Holy God invites us to join in—to be wholly invested in these holy plans.

When we accept our calling to be holy, we not only participate in the recreating of this world, we also participate in the recreating of us. By accepting our invitation to be holy, we welcome the change within us. God grows, stretches, and transforms us through this calling.

So embrace holiness. Claim holiness. Head towards holiness. Reflect God's holiness. Listen to the yearning deep inside of you. Become who God is making you. Be where God is placing you. Go where God is guiding you. And in doing this you will discover who you are, where you belong, and why you are here.

Be holy.

Find identity.

Find belonging.

Find purpose.

epilogue

Hans Küng—Swiss Catholic priest, theologian, and prolific author—wrote this statement in the introduction to his book, *On Being a Christian*: "This book was written, not because the author thinks he is a good Christian, but because he thinks that being a Christian is a particularly good thing."[1]

I did not write this book because I think I am good at being holy.

I wrote it because I think our calling to be holy is a very good thing.

I do not have holiness all figured out. I am not 100 percent confident in who I am, where I belong, or why I am here. I will never fully understand my calling, my identity, my belonging, or my purpose. But I think these are things worth pursuing.

Because when you commit to being wholly holy, you begin to live the life you were created to live. You become grounded in a brighter world. You find fulfillment in a better way. Your yearnings are met. Your cravings are satisfied. Your thirst is quenched. Your desire is transformed. And your quest begins.

So I will continually strive to live into this scriptural command—to be holy—and I am asking you to come with me on this journey. What I have tried to do in this book is convince you that being holy is a good thing, give you some practical ways to get started, and encourage you to discover the rest along the way. So now I invite you.

Join me.

Find identity, find belonging, find purpose.

Be holy.

notes

preface

[1]NRSV, 1 Peter 1:15-16

[2]NRSV, Ephesians 1:4

[3]NRSV, Revelation 22:11

[4]Rodger Nishioka, *The Roots of Who We Are* (Louisville: Bridge Resources, 1997).

[5]David Kinnaman and Gabe Lyons, *UnChristian: What a New Generation Really Thinks About Christianity ... And Why It Matters* (Grand Rapids, MI: Baker Books, 2007).

[6]Kenda Creasy Dean, *Almost Christian: What The Faith of Our Teenagers Is Telling the American Church* (New York: Oxford University Press, 2010).

chapter 1—yearning

[1]You can actually watch this on youtube.com. Do a search for "Joshua Bell Washington Post."

[2]Calculated by dividing the total revolving debt in the U.S. ($801.0 billion) by the estimated number of households carrying credit card debt (50.2 million)—from the December 2011 data as listed in the Federal Reserve's February 2012 report on consumer credit.

[3]See http.//www.daveramsey.com/fpu/home.

[4]William James, *The Principles of Psychology* (New York: Dover Publications, 1918), 462.

[5]*Vanity Fair* magazine (April 1991 issue).

[6]Vulgate, Luke 2:29–32

[7]NRSV, Luke 2:29–32

[8]I first heard this comparison in one of Tim Keller's sermons. They are brilliant and inspiring and available for download at http://sermons2.redeemer.com/.

chapter 2—become

[1]See www.pinterest.com.

[2]NRSV, Leviticus 20:7

[3]NRSV, Luke 2:23

[4]NRSV, 1 Corinthians 7:14

[5]NRSV, Exodus 29:21

[6]NRSV, Numbers 6:5

[7]NRSV, Leviticus 21:8

[8]NRSV, Leviticus 21:6

[9]Tickle said this in her sermon "A Treasure We Don't Understand" to Mars Hill Bible Church on May 3, 2009.

[10]NRSV, John 15:5

[11]NRSV, Romans 11:16

[12]NRSV, Ephesians 1:4

[13]NRSV, Colossians 1:21–22

[14]CEB, 1 Corinthians 6:11

[15]CEB, 1 Corinthians 1:30–31

[16]NRSV, 1 Peter 1:15-16

[17]An infinitive aorist passive verb is a continuous verb.

[18]Kenda Creasy Dean, *Almost Christian: What The Faith Of Our Teenagers Is Telling The American Church* (New York: Oxford University Press, 2010), 65.

chapter 3—reflection

[1]NIV, Isaiah 1:18

[2]F. Brown, S. Driver, and C. Briggs, *The Brown-Driver-Briggs Hebrew and English Lexicon* (London: Bagster, 1976).

[3]See http://myholysmoke.com.

[4]Leander E. Keck, *The New Interpreter's Bible: Volume 1* (Nashville: Abingdon Press, 1998).

[5]NIV, Leviticus 20:26

[6]Notice I said "some." The overwhelming majority of the Kenyan preachers I met were nothing like this and are amazing, inspiring, faithful servant-leaders who joyfully proclaim the true good news of the gospel.

[7]Walter Brueggemann, *Theology of the Old Testament: testimony, dispute, advocacy* (Minneapolis: Fortress Press, 1997), 288–93.

[8]See http://holysmokesbatman.com/directory.

[9]NRSV, Matthew 19:28

[10]NRSV, Colossians 1:20

[11]NRSV, Acts 3:21

[12]NRSV, Leviticus 8:24

[13]Richard Boyce, *Westminster Bible Companion: Leviticus and Numbers* (Louisville: Westminster John Knox Press, 2008) 59–60.

[14]NRSV, Leviticus 19:2

[15]Walter Brueggemann, *Holiness: From the Bible to Today* (Louisville: Thoughtful Christian, 2013).

[16]"Refiner's Fire," by Brian Doerksen. Copyright © 1990.

chapter 4—lost

[1]This conversation in the movie contains a few more words and is a little more PG-13. I edited and paraphrased parts of it for our purposes here.

[2]"Nope, I'm a frayed knot" sounds just like "Nope, I'm afraid not." It's not funny if I have to explain it to you.

[3]This analogy was not unique to him - it has been used a lot. It is even referenced in Martin Luther King's "Letter from Birmingham Jail."

[4]Jay Walker-Smith, Yankelovich Consumer Research

[5]Statistic comes from a study done by *Advertising Age* and available for download at http://gaia.adage.com/images/random/datacenter/2008/spendtrends08.pdf.

[6]NRSV, Mark 8:27

[7]NRSV, Malachi 4:5

[8]NRSV, Mark 8:29

[9]NRSV, Mark 8:29

[10]John Calvin, *Institutes of the Christian Religion* (Boston: MobileReference.com, 2010) book 1, chapter 1, parts 1-2.

[11]NRSV, Mark 8:29

[12]NRSV, Deuteronomy 7:6

[13]NRSV, 1 Corinthians 3:17

[14]NRSV, 1 Peter 2:4–5

chapter 5—beloved

[1]See http://www.ted.com/talks/thandie_newton_embracing_otherness_embracing_myself.html

[2]NRSV, Jeremiah 1:5

[3]NRSV, Matthew 10:30

[4]NRSV, 1 Chronicles 28:21, 29:3

[5]NRSV, John 4:26

[6]Barbara Brown Taylor, "Identity Confirmation," *Christian Century* (February 28, 1996).

[7]Max Lucado, *You Are Special* (Wheaton, IL: Crossway Books, 1997).

[8]Brennan Manning, *Abba's Child: The Cry of the Heart for Intimate Belonging* (Colorado Springs: NavPress, 2002).

[9]NRSV, Isaiah 43:1–4a

[10]NRSV, Ephesians 2:4–5,10

[11]Henri Nouwen, *Life of the Beloved: Spiritual Living in a Secular World* (New York: Crossroad, 1992), 27.

[12]Ibid.

[13]NRSV, Romans 8:38–39

[14]NRSV, Colossians 3:12

chapter 6—identify

[1]*Mirriam-Webster Learner's Dictionary*

[2]NRSV, 1 Thessalonians 4:7

[3]NRSV, John 17:11,16

[4]NRSV, Hebrews 7:26 and Matthew 11:19

[5]NRSV, Romans 12:2

[6]NRSV, Deuteronomy 31:6

[7]Oscar Wilde, *De Profundis* (Champaign, IL: Project Gutenberg, 1897).

[8]NRSV, Psalm 139:14

[9]Maya Angelou, *I Know why the Caged Bird Sings* (New York: Bantam Books, 1971), 154.

[10]NRSV, 1 Timothy 4:14

[11]NRSV, Romans 12:6

[12]NIV, 1 Peter 4:10

[13]Stanley Saunders, *The Word on the Street: Performing the Scriptures in the Urban Context* (Grand Rapids: WM. B. Eerdmans Pub., 2000), 42.

[14]NIV, Mark 1:11

[15]NRSV, Exodus 20:8

[16]NRSV, Deuteronomy 5:12

[17]Walter Brueggemann, *Journey to the Common Good* (Louisville: Westminster John Knox Press, 2010), 26.

[18]NIV, Hebrews 4:9–11

chapter 7—loneliness

[1]Robert Putnam, *Bowling Alone: The Collapse and Revival of American Community* (New York: Simon and Schuster, 2000).

[2]Paul Tillich, *The Courage to Be* (New Haven, CT: Yale University Press. 1952).

[3]See http://www.guardian.co.uk/film/2010/mar/27/drew-barrymore-interview

[4]Edgar Allen Poe "From Childhood's Hour," in *Complete Stories and Poems* (Garden City, NY: Doubleday, 1966), 812.

[5]Douglas Coupland, *Miss Wyoming* (New York: Pantheon Books, 1999).

[6]See http://us.blizzard.com/en-us/company/press/pressreleases.html?101007

[7]See http://www.goodreads.com/quotes/

[8]NRSV, 1 Corinthians 12:12

[9]NRSV, 1 Corinthians 12:12

[10]NRSV, 1 Corinthians 12:14

[11]NRSV, 1 Corinthians 12:15–17

[12]NRSV, 1 Corinthians 12:19

[13]NRSV, Ephesians 2:19-22

chapter 8—communal

[1]World Alliance of YMCAs, "Blue Book" (Retrieved 2012-07-23).

[2]NRSV, Genesis 1-2

[3]NRSV, Genesis 2:18

[4]NRSV, Genesis 2:18

[5]NRSV, Genesis 2:18

[6]NRSV, Genesis 2:18
[7]NRSV, Genesis 2:20
[8]NRSV, Genesis 2:23
[9]NRSV, 2 Corinthians 7:3
[10]NRSV, 1 Peter 3:8
[11]NRSV, Psalm 133:1
[12]NRSV, Hebrews 3:1
[13]NRSV, Exodus 19:6
[14]NRSV, Joel 3:17
[15]NRSV, Isaiah 62:12
[16]NRSV, Deuteronomy 7:6, 14:2, 26:19
[17]NRSV, Galatians 3:28
[18]NRSV, 1 Peter 2:5
[19]NRSV, Ephesians 5:27
[20]NRSV, Genesis 2:18
[21]NIV, Genesis 4:2
[22]NIV, Genesis 4:2
[23]NRSV, Ephesians 4:1–3
[24]Donald Miller gives a cool illustration really close to this at the end of his book *A Million Miles in a Thousand Years: What I Learned While Editing My Life* (Nashville: Thomas Nelson, 2009).
[25]NRSV, Revelation 21:1–2

chapter 9—connect

[1]Stanley Hauerwas, "The Gesture of a Truthful Story," *Theology Today* (July 1985).
[2]NRSV, Mat 18:21–35
[3]NRSV, Mat 18:21–35
[4]Even if Nelson Mandela did not say these exact words, Morgan Freeman did when he played Nelson Mandela in the 2009 movie *Invictus*—cool movie.
[5]NRSV, Luke 15:3
[6]NRSV, Luke 15:20
[7]NRSV, Luke 15:23–24
[8]Timothy Keller, *The Prodigal God: Recovering the Heart of the Christian Faith* (New York: Penguin Group, 2008), 1.
[9]This was taken from the "Democratic presidential candidates debate" in Iowa on 8/19/07, which can be viewed at https://www.youtube.com/watch?v=NMVKnlqls6M
[10]Sara Miles, *Jesus Freak: Feeding, Healing, Raising the Dead* (San Francisco: Jossey-Bass, 2010), 85.
[11]This is a portion the "Prayer for the Eucharistic Adoration" by Pope John Paul II.
[12]NRSV, Malachi 2:10
[13]See http://www.ted.com/talks/brene_brown_on_vulnerability.html
[14]Brené Brown, *The Gifts of Imperfection: Let Go of Who You Think You're Supposed To Be and Embrace Who You Are* (Center City, MN: Hazelden, 2010), 49.

chapter 10—aimless

[1]Lewis Carroll, *Alice's Adventures in Wonderland* (London: Collier-Macmillan). 75.
[2]Søren Kierkegaard, *Repetition: An Essay In Experimental Psychology* (Princeton, NJ: Princeton University Press 1941), 114.
[3]Thomas Merton, *Thoughts in Solitude* (New York: Farrar, Straus & Cudahy 1958).
[4]Viktor Frankl, *Man's Search for Meaning* (Boston: Beacon Press 2006), 104.
[5]*GQ* magazine (January 2011).
[6]NIV, Matthew 7:7–8 …but instead of "search(es)" I used the more familiar "seek(s)"
[7]NRSV, Romans 1:1

chapter 11—balance

[1]NRSV, Matthew 22:36
[2]NRSV, Matthew 22:37–40
[3]NRSV, Matthew 22:37
[4]NRSV, Matthew 22:39
[5]NRSV, Matthew 22:39
[6]NIV, Deuteronomy 6:4–5
[7]NIV, Deuteronomy 6:6-9
[8]NRSV, Numbers 15:40
[9]The Westminster Shorter Catechism, question 1.
[10]NRSV, Romans 11:36
[11]NRSV, Revelation 4:11
[12]NRSV, 1 Corinthians 10:31
[13]NRSV, Psalm 144:15
[14]NRSV, Luke 2:10
[15]NRSV, Philippians 4:4
[16]Rick Warren in his sermon "What Makes God Smile?"
[17]NRSV, Luke 10:29
[18]NRSV, Luke 10:36
[19]NIV, John 10:11
[20]NIV, John 6:35
[21]John 8:12, 10:9, 15:5, 11:25
[22]NIV, Philippians 2:4
[23]NRSV, Luke 10:35
[24]NRSV, Luke 10:37
[25]NRSV, Luke 10:37
[26]NIV, Matthew 7:12
[27]Udana-Varga 5:18
[28]Mahabharata 5:5157
[29]Talmud, Shabbat 31a
[30]Analects 15:23
[31]Dadistan-i-dinik 94:5
[32]Hadith of an-Nawawi 13
[33]T'ai Shang Kan Ying P'ien
[34]NRSV, Job 31:6
[35]NRSV, Proverbs 19:2
[36]NIV, James 1:22

chapter 12—embrace

[1]See http://www.toms.com/
[2]NRSV, Ephesians 4:22,24
[3]NRSV, Ephesians 4:25–32
[4]NRSV, Ephesians 4:24
[5]NRSV, Luke 10:37
[6]NRSV, Micah 6:8
[7]NRSV, Luke 4:18–19
[8]NRSV, Matthew 28:19–20
[9]NRSV, Matthew 28:20
[10]Marcus Buckingham, *The Truth About You: Your Secret to Success* (Nashville: Thomas Nelson, 2008), 39.
[11]See http://www.npr.org/2011/07/09/137348637in-uganda-american-becomes-foster-mom-to-13-girls

[12]Donald Miller, *A Million Miles in a Thousand Years: What I Learned While Editing My Life* (Nashville: Thomas Nelson, 2009), 248.

[13]Hélder Câmara, *Spiral of Violence* (London: Sheed and Ward, 1971).

epilogue

[1]Hans Küng, *On Being a Christian* (Garden City, NY: Doubleday, 1976).